Natural Gourmet Cooking by

swissair ✚

Welcome

to Swissair's "Natural Gourmet Cooking."

I am delighted that you are holding our cookbook in your hands. As we were putting together this colourful, lively and unconventional book of recipes, we were thinking of everyone who appreciates the quality of our naturalgourmet catering line or who is curious about the creations of the famous chefs who took part in our venture. And of everyone who wants eating and drinking to be a healthy, natural and enjoyable experience, whether on board an aircraft or at home. In short, we were thinking of you.

Let yourself be swept away on this culinary journey. I hope it brings you not only fun, but also exciting new taste sensations. You'll see: "Natural Gourmet Cooking" is the most natural thing in the world.

It would be our great pleasure to be able to treat you to naturalgourmet on board.

Jeffrey G. Katz
President and CEO of Swissair

The Biography of a Great Idea: naturalgourmet

It was summer and quite hot, and if one had been a fly on the wall, one would have heard a discussion that was also pretty heated. It concerned developments and trends in gastronomy – and what kinds of opportunities they could mean for Swissair. And then it was there. Spontaneously and unexpectedly. The idea of switching the entire food and beverage section over as completely as possible to ecologically sound products was fascinating. It was new – really new. Because up until then, no other airline had taken on this idea with all its consequences.

But would it work? How would passengers react to it? How could available resources to produce over 60,000 ecologically sound meals daily be found in Switzerland alone? How would the Swiss organic farming industry cope with such high demand? What did this mean for foreign producers? Where would Swissair get 2 million organic eggs? Where would 200,000 litres of organic orange juice come from? Where can you find 1.6 million litres of organic milk? And what about coffee, beer and baby food? What principles apply to acquisition, transportation and other ecological aspects? How could the changeover be accomplished? A thousand questions – and otherwise nothing but the certainty that it was a great idea, one which would also bring with it obstacles and challenges.

First came the idea, and then came the hard work. A lot of know-how had to be acquired. Specialists from the fields of gastronomy, logistics and marketing, as well as representatives from the Swiss Consumer Organisation and the organic farming industry were called in as consultants. Market studies clarified the acceptance of the undertaking, suppliers and producers at home and abroad had to be contacted, guidelines had to be formulated, and a step-by-step plan for the changeover had to be established. And last but not least, there was the task of creating menus for this innovative catering concept. The renowned Swiss chefs Roland Jöhri and Wolfgang Kuchler developed the new gourmet line with Swissair's own staff and created recipes for it: naturalgourmet was born. That all happened in 1996.

On June 3, 1997, it was time: the introduction of naturalgourmet on all Swissair flights out of Zurich and Geneva! Of course, it would have been preferable to be able switch the whole inflight catering operation over at once, but that was logistically impossible. Doing it in phases guaranteed a more serious approach and was at the same time a confirmation of Swissair's long-term commitment to the naturalgourmet catering concept. And it would eventually be implemented on as much of Swissair's route network as possible, not just Zurich and Geneva. By the end of 1998, when the changeover in Zurich and Geneva is completed, the concept will be expanded to other catering operations abroad.

For over a year now, naturalgourmet has proven itself a success with both passengers and personnel – the reactions to it have been overwhelmingly positive and demonstrate that naturalgourmet is the consistent extension of one fundamental objective: the well-being of Swissair passengers. For those who fly on up to 200 days a year, as many of our customers do, on-board meals are an important element in the overall nutritional picture. And if this element is not only healthy and natural, but also a culinary treat, then naturalgourmet has succeeded in creating a symbiosis between real customer needs and environmental awareness.

The pioneering phase is now concluded. With the publication of this unconventional cookbook, the authors, with the help of internationally famous chef Anton Mosimann and Peter Roth, world champion in drink mixing, present a cookbook that allows naturalgourmet to become a private cooking and eating experience as well. Over 120 simple but sophisticated recipes have been created by our catering staff, who were inspired, among others, by culinary influences from Switzerland, the Far East and the Mediterranean – and who have come up with a host of new culinary discoveries. Welcome on board with naturalgourmet!

Our commitment

- naturalgourmet is a healthy culinary treat – and it is ethically and ecologically responsible.
- We are committed to having 90% of all products used on board from inspected organic sources and integrated production operations by the year 2001.
- We use, wherever possible, meat from farms that adhere to natural-environment holding conditions for livestock.
- We offer more meatless meal alternatives.
- We take into consideration the seasonal nature of products.
- We practice fair trade.
- We avoid, reduce or recycle waste and use biodegradable materials wherever possible.
- We have our production operations inspected by organizations that are certified by IFOAM (International Federation of Organic Agriculture Movements).

It wasn't raining when Noah built the ark

But that fact and the fact that everyone thought Noah was crazy didn't stop the flood – it came as it had to come, and with considerable force.

Translated, that means that first of all, crazy people are right now and then, and second, that there are developments that can't be stopped. And third, that it's usually a good idea to think ahead.

Not that we in the naturalgourmet team would think of comparing ourselves with the visionary figure Noah. Or that we have created a similarly paradisiacal ark with naturalgourmet. Certainly not. We simply tried to appraise developments and to match them to certain needs, wishes and desires. And because one is what one eats, as Brillat-Savarin said, we started there. Happier products, happier passengers.

Life is relatively simple. As is a true gourmet kitchen. "The Physiology of Taste," I believe, begins in the pasture or in the stall, because natural products taste better. They smell of sun and of life, and have an identity and a uniqueness. The palate recognises this, and the delicate taste sensors rejoice – especially when the preparation is also right. It doesn't have to be complicated. The authors of this cookbook prove that. The recipes are not sacrosanct, but are meant to inspire you to experiment and discover your own lively variations. Life is relatively simple – but at the same time as colourful as a butterfly and full of innumerable exciting possibilities. That's true of cooking, too. Trying out new dishes, playing around with the preparation, combining different ingredients, taking a risk – even if it leads to a flop – those are the things that will help you discover new tastes. There are many interpretations of Noah's Ark. My own is perhaps this: saving something that is in danger of being lost – in this case, the capacity to trust our own creativity and ability.

Cuno Blattner

Cuno Blattner
Gastronome and "godfather" of naturalgourmet

Table of contents

Notes on the Recipes

- If not otherwise indicated, recipes are calculated for 4 people
- We have used the usual household sizes for measuring units. Converted, this translates into

1 tbsp.   15ml

1 tsp.   5ml

100 ml   equals 1dl or ¹⁄₁₀ litre

weight/solids		volume/liquids	
15g	½oz	15ml	½fl oz (1tbsp)
25g	1oz	25ml	1fl oz
35g	1½oz	35ml	1½fl oz (2tbsp)
50g	2oz	50ml	2fl oz (3tbsp)
75g	3oz	75ml	3fl oz (4tbsp)
100g	3½oz	100ml	3½fl oz
125g	4½oz	125ml	4½fl oz
150g	5½oz	150ml	5½fl oz
175g	6oz	175ml	6fl oz
200g	7oz	200ml	7fl oz
225g	8oz	225ml	8fl oz
250g	9oz	250ml (¼l)	9fl oz
275g	9½oz	275ml	9½fl oz
300g	10oz	300ml	10fl oz (½pint)
325g	11½oz	325ml	11½fl oz
350g	12oz	350ml	12fl oz
375g	13oz	375ml	13fl oz
400g	14oz	400ml	14fl oz
425g	15oz	425ml	15fl oz
450g	1lb	450ml	16fl oz
500g	1lb 2oz	500ml (½l)	18fl oz
600g	1lb 4oz	600ml	20fl oz (1pint)
700g	1lb 9oz	700ml	1¼ pints
750g	1lb 10oz	750ml (¾l)	26fl oz
800g	1lb 12oz	800ml	28fl oz
900g	2lb	900ml	32fl oz
1kg	2lb 4oz	1litre	1¾ pints
1.25kg	2lb 12oz	1.25litres	2 pints
1.5kg	3lb 5oz	1.5litres	2¾ pints
2kg	4lb 8oz	2litres	3½ pints
2.25kg	5lb	2.25litres	4 pints
2.5kg	5lb 8oz	2.5litres	4½ pints
3kg	6lb 8oz	3litres	5¼ pints

- Use fresh, seasonal products – experiment in winter with apples instead of fresh raspberries or apricots, or with leeks instead of summer peas. And of course the other way around!
- Recipes are never unassailable – allow your imagination free rein, discover new variations, and make your own creations; trust your sense of taste and your inclinations!
- If certain kinds of fish are not available, try the recipe using another favourite fish or ask your fish merchant for a suggestion.
- Instead of gelatine, try using plant-based agar-agar. Follow the preparation instructions on the package.
- Go on a voyage of discovery! Where can you buy produce direct from the farmer? Where and when are there outdoor markets with fresh products? Where is the nearest organic foods market or health-food store? Be inquisitive and pepper the staff with questions – even difficult ones!
- If you buy organic or fair-trade products when you shop, you not only support independent, small-scale farmers, but also promote responsible, natural and sustainable farming techniques.
- At the end of this book you will find the addresses of suppliers and organisations where you can get further information. In addition, naturalgourmet has founded its own product line, which is based primarily on organic, natural products. You will also find more information about this at the end of the book.

Brunch at the Montreux Palace

TAKE OFF FOR A WEEKEND.

Leave your worries behind

and enjoy everything – relax

and time out. Celebrate the

lushness of the world. Let

your growing lighthearted

run free – and discover the

new day in a carefree mood.

WELCOME FOR BRUNCH.

Awakening
Metamorphosis and transcendence – a happy state of being between two worlds, wrapped in the cocoon of dreams,

yet the new day is only the flutter of a wing away: Bon voyage and the best of luck in your adventure of awakening.

Indulge yourself in grandeur

Indulge yourself in grandeur and a sense of warmth and security. Both on the ground and in the air, Swiss hospitality has a long-standing tradition – whether on board an aircraft or in the rich tradition of luxury hotels. And like the pioneers of aviation, the Swiss hotel pioneers also had powerful visions, the courage to take risks, and an untamed belief in the possible: In the space of a few decades, Cäsar Ritz built an international hotel empire; with their legendary hotels, the Bon, Seiler and Badrutt family dynasties laid the foundation in the early 19th century for Switzerland's reputation as a vacation paradise. The turn of the century was the grand era of hotels, the economy flourished – especially that of the British Empire – and a grow-

ing mobility brought the international créme de la créme from one elegant resort to another. In the gleam-ing hotel halls of Monte Carlo, London,

St. Petersburg and New York, dizzyingly glamourous parties were held; in the Swiss Alps, the "beautiful people" met for winter sports or for summer relaxation; and at the spas, one joined one's friends for a cure.

Still today, some of this exuberant worldliness is evident when the names of great hotels are mentioned – names like "Badrutt's Palace" in St. Moritz, the "Hotel Seiler" in Zermatt, the "Grand Hotel National" in Lucerne, the "Beau Rivage" in Lausanne, the "Grand Hotel Victoria-Jungfrau" in Interlaken or the "Quellenhof" in Bad Ragaz. In spite of all the ups and downs of world history, they have all maintained their charm and style and continue to weave the fabric that (hotel) dreams are made of.

Questions for eggheads

Do you slice the top off or crack and peel your soft-boiled egg? What does that say about you? Are you sure? Do you know the chickens whose eggs you eat? Why not? Do you know a chicken that lays golden eggs? Did you ever work for chicken feed? Did you enjoy it? Are you chicken-hearted? About what? When did you last have a (chicken) bone to pick? With whom? How many eggs have you eaten in your lifetime? And how many chickens? Do you consider yourself an egghead? What, in your opinion, is a perfect egg? Do you think that people can be as similar to each other as two eggs? How similar is one egg to another? What do you think came first, the chicken or the egg? Why?

One of the grand old ladies of Swiss hotel history is the "Montreux Palace Hotel," which today is part of the international "Swissôtel" chain of the SAir Group.

The imposing turn-of-the-century establishment is located right on the shores of Lake Geneva, between palm trees and the snowy peaks of the Dents-du-Midi. The Grand Old Lady, confident and independent, elegantly combines the past with the future. Whether in the Petit Palais, on the terrace, or in the grandiose Salle de fête, the great era of the fin de siècle and its high art of hospitality are obvious both to the eyes and the senses – even more so since the present has added its own attributes, including more space and convenience.

Prune Compote

400g prunes
1 cinnamon stick
pared zest of 1 lemon
300g caster sugar

1 Soak the prunes in warm water to cover for 24 hours.

2 Put the soaked prunes in a pan with the soaking water, the cinnamon stick, lemon zest and sugar and bring to a boil. Simmer gently for 10 minutes, then allow to cool. Remove the cinnamon and lemon zest. Serve well chilled.

Fresh Figs in Red Wine

1 litre red wine
250g caster sugar
1 cinnamon stick
4–5 cloves
juice of 2 lemons
12 black figs
1 orange

1 Put the wine in a pan with the sugar, cinnamon, cloves and lemon juice and simmer for 10 minutes. Wipe the figs with a damp cloth, add to the pan and poach gently for 10 minutes. Lift them out and put them in a serving dish. Boil the wine down to reduce to a third of its volume, pour it over the figs and allow them to cool. Refrigerate until needed.

2 Cut away the peel and pith from the oranges with a sharp knife, right down to the flesh. Cut out the segments of flesh from between the membranes. To serve, quarter the figs and arrange the orange segments on top.

Birchermüesli

125g rolled oats
200ml milk
4 tbsp caster sugar
2 tbsp honey
500g red apples
500g mixed fruit in season (apricots, peaches, nectarines, soft fruit)
2 bananas
2 oranges
3 tbsp whipping cream, well chilled
juice of 2 lemons
50g ground hazelnuts
25g walnuts, roughly chopped

1 Soak the oats in the milk with the sugar and honey and chill for 4 hours. Grate the unpeeled apple. Prepare the remaining fruit and cut in small cubes depending on size and sort. Set aside some fruit to garnish the Müesli. Beat the cream stiffly.

2 Mix together all the ingredients. Fold in the cream carefully and taste the Müesli. Garnish with the reserved fruit.

French Toast

Peach Jam

500g peaches
400g caster sugar
juice of ½ lemon
2 cloves
3 tbsp white wine
2 tbsp water

1 Plunge the peaches in boiling water for 2 minutes, peel, halve and cut them in small pieces. Put in a glass bowl, sprinkle with sugar and leave for 12 hours.

2 Put the peaches in a preserving pan with all the remaining ingredients and bring to a boil, stirring. Cook until setting point is reached. Fish out the cloves and pour the jam into jam jars. For best keeping qualities, the jam should be put into hot jars and covered while still hot.

Tip:
Peach jam can also be flavoured with ginger, peppercorns or whisky.

1 Mix together the eggs and milk. Dip each of the toast slices in the egg-milk mixture. Heat the butter in a non-stick frying pan and fry the slices gently on both sides.

2 Mix together the sugar and cinnamon on a plate and turn the toast slices in it. Serve warm, sprinkled if wished with icing sugar. Serve maple syrup separately.

Tip:
An apricot compote goes well with this dish.

18

Eggs Bénédictine

100g young spinach leaves
200ml hollandaise sauce
(see recipe page 193)
4 ready-baked vol-au-vent cases
100ml white wine vinegar
4 large newly laid eggs
4 half slices ham
25g butter
salt and freshly ground pepper

Tip:
The acidity of the vinegar helps to keep the eggs together while poaching. Salt has the opposite effect, so do not salt the water.

1 Trim and wash the spinach, drain well. Prepare the hollandaise sauce and keep it warm. Heat the vol-au-vent cases and keep them warm.

2 Bring a shallow pan of water to a simmer and add the vinegar. Break the eggs one by one into a cup and slide them carefully into the barely simmering water. Poach them for 4–5 minutes, lift them out, rinse carefully in hot water and keep them warm.

3 Meanwhile, heat the butter in a large pan and sweat the spinach gently in it until just wilted. Divide the spinach between the vol-au-vent cases. Toss the ham slices in a little hot butter and lay them on top of the spinach. Finish with the poached eggs and hollandaise sauce.

8 slices white bread
4 eggs
200ml milk
50g butter
125g caster sugar
a little cinnamon

icing sugar
100ml maple syrup

Swiss Plaited Milk Loaf and Rye bread (see basic recipe page 190)

Omelette Freiburg-Style

8 eggs
salt and freshly ground pepper
50g butter
100g Vacherin Fribourgeois cheese, cubed
1 tomato, peeled, seeded and diced
herbs to garnish, optional

1 Beat the eggs two by two and season them. Heat an omelette pan and melt a little butter in it. Make four omelettes, adding to each one a quarter of the cheese. Stir occasionally with a fork,

continually bringing the outer edges into the middle until the omelette starts to set. The centre should remain soft. Tip the pan and roll the omelette over. Serve on warmed plates. Toss the tomato dice in a little hot butter, season. Make an incision in the top of the omelettes and fill with the tomato dice. Garnish if wished with herbs.

Guinea Fowl Pancakes

Pancake mixture:
75g wholewheat flour
75g plain white flour
4 eggs
250ml milk
3 tbsp whipping cream
25g butter
salt and freshly ground pepper, nutmeg

1 guinea fowl breast, about 200g
2 tbsp oil
150ml chicken stock
200g flat-leaved parsley and a little chervil and lovage, if available
50g chilled butter
200g oyster mushrooms, medium or large
25g butter

1 Blend together all the ingredients for the pancakes and leave to rest for half an hour.

2 Season the guinea fowl breast and sear in hot oil; it should remain a little pink inside. Remove and keep it warm. Drain away any excess fat and deglaze the pan with the stock. Bring to a boil, add the chopped parsley and other herbs and simmer together briefly. Season, blend until smooth in the liquidiser.

3 Slice the mushrooms and fry them in the butter. Season to taste.

4 Make 8 thin pancakes in a small crêpe pan. Cut the guinea fowl breast in 8 slices and wrap each one in a pancake. Reheat the sauce gently and work in the chilled butter bit by bit. Serve the pancakes with the mushrooms and pour the parsley sauce over.

Leek Quiche à la Vaudoise

For an 18cm-diameter quiche tin

200g shortcrust pastry (see recipe page 193)
250g leeks
125g Vaudois sausage (or other smoked boiling sausage)
50g butter
150ml whipping cream
2 eggs
50g Gruyère, grated
salt and freshly ground pepper
nutmeg

1 Butter the quiche tin and line it with the rolled out pastry. Leave to rest for at least an hour.

2 Cut the leeks in chunks, sweat them in half the butter. Season to taste, cover and cook gently for 5 minutes. Allow them to cool. Cut the sausage in chunks and fry gently for 5 minutes in the remaining butter.

3 Heat the oven to 220ºC/Gas 6. Whisk together the cream and the eggs. Add the grated cheese, salt, pepper and nutmeg. Put the leeks and sausage pieces in the pastry case and pour over the egg mixture. Bake for about 30 minutes.

Baked Eggs with Chanterelles

75g chanterelles
25g butter + a little extra for buttering the
ramekins
4 tbsp whipping cream
4 large eggs
salt and freshly ground pepper
4 sprigs chervil or borage flowers

1 Trim and clean the chanterelles and if
necessary quarter or chop them up small. Sweat
them in a small pan with 25g butter. Season to taste,
add the cream.

2 Butter 4 ovenproof ramekins generously
and divide the chanterelles between them. Break an
egg into each one. Put the ramekins in a baking tin
or shallow pan and add hot water to come halfway
up the sides. Cover and bring the water to a simmer
on top of the stove. Continue cooking until the
whites are set and the yolks still soft. Sprinkle with
salt and pepper and garnish with a sprig of chervil or
borage flowers.

Tip:
Toasted coun-
try bread
goes well
with this dish.

'Poularde de Gruyère' with leeks and potatoes

a 1.4kg oven-ready chicken
a bouquet garni (thyme, rosemary,
bay leaf)
400g leeks
400g potatoes
oil
150g finely diced carrots, celeriac
and onions
25g butter
600ml whipping cream
salt and freshly ground pepper
nutmeg

Bernese Rösti Potatoes

800g firm, waxy potatoes
1 medium onion
50g smoked streaky bacon
3–4 tbsp clarified butter or a mixture of
butter and oil
salt and pepper

1 A day before you plan to make the rösti, cook the unpeeled potatoes in boiling salted water for about 10 minutes. They should remain quite firm. Drain, cool them a little, skin and refrigerate them. The next day grate them coarsely. Chop the onion and cut the bacon in small dice. Soften the onion and bacon in half the butter (or butter and oil) without allowing the onion to brown. Mix them with the grated potatoes and season to taste. Add the rest of the butter (or butter and oil) to the pan and let it get good and hot. Add the potatoes, bacon and onions, press them together into a flat cake, reduce the heat and fry until golden brown on both sides.

1 Season the chicken with salt and pepper. Put the bouquet garni inside the cavity. Slice the leeks and cut the potatoes in small cubes.

2 Brown the chicken on all sides over moderate heat in hot oil. Remove and keep it warm. Brown the carrots, celeriac and onions in the same pan. Drain off the fat, moisten with 300ml water and boil down hard to reduce to a quarter. Strain and season to taste.

3 Sweat the leeks gently in butter, add the cream and the potato cubes and cook over moderate heat, stirring occasionally, for about 20 minutes. Season to taste.

4 Carve the chicken into 8 pieces. Divide the leeks and potatoes between serving plates, arrange 2 pieces of chicken over each serving and pour over the gravy.

SR 100

ZURICH-NEW YORK

AIR TRAVEL – TIME TRAVEL between slow and fast. Oscillating between time

and speed, between different rhythms of the body and the spirit: stationary

while moving over the clouds at 900 kilometres per hour; the feeling of being

at a standstill contradicting the knowledge of the physical dynamics; here the aimless chain of thought in your head,

spinning and turning in spirals, there the

destination-driven flight path of the jet,

linear and calculable. Irritating, these

simultaneous inconsistencies of realisation,

sensation and knowledge, and nevertheless

precious, this double experience that will

dissolve at the very latest in the

stream of our familiar world upon landing.

What remains? What was there before?

when it has come

marches on

heals all wounds

stands still

to go

is wasted

it is time

is won

time

is taken

longest

is given

exact

what a!

is whiled away

is turned back –

time

the times of our life

the right

the tines of our life

hard ones

bad ones

better ones

time

Swissair

1952

1952. It was legendary: The first overseas air connection from the little airport in Zurich long time ago, and it was a long time before the DC-4, a four-engine propeller aircraft carrying storms, making five or more intermediate stops from Tenerife to the ice deserts of Newfound flight. They were long hours, if comfortable ones, spent in berths and enjoyed at tables set the galley, the breakfast menu also catering to individual wishes and preferences guests and familiar faces among the staff. Everyone was happy and greeted each business leaders and politicians – could choose their own captain and crew pleasant flight. For Swissair, it meant one more brick for building its soon-to

HB-ILA • SWISS AIR LINES

Swissair

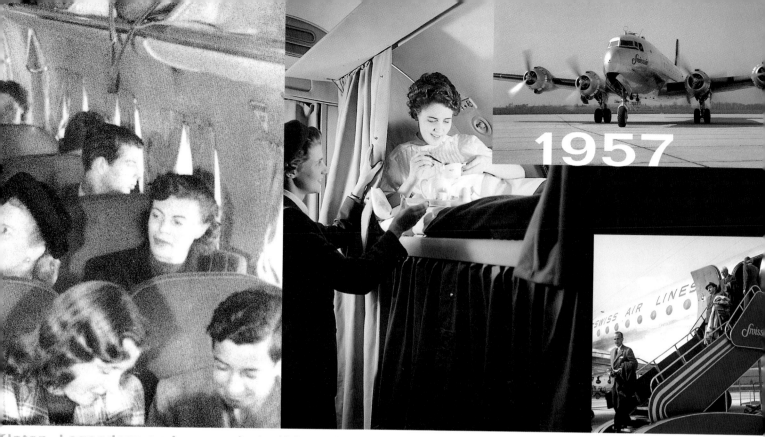

1957

Kloten. Legendary and somewhat elitist, since one needed time and even more money. It was a
4 passengers – always flying with the air currents over the ocean and, depending on wind and
and – could finally take a bearing on the glimmering skyline of New York after a 26-hour
with silver, the stewards in white tuxedos serving and flambéing, cooking done à la minute in
t least in First Class. An airplane? It was more like a small flying hotel, with many regular
ther heartily and by name, because all the frequent flyers of that era – stars and royalty,
which was a compliment for the crew and meant that the passengers could anticipate a
e-famous reputation.

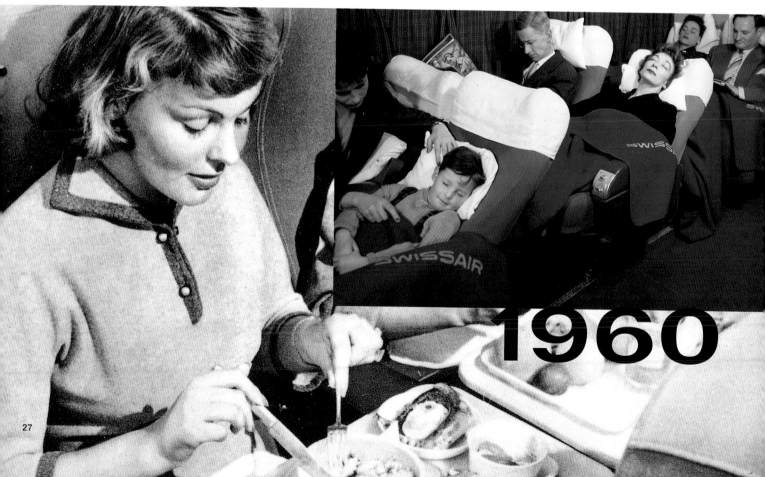

1960

2000

The legendary Swiss hospitality of that time played a role in forming the character of today's Swissair. Quality service and customer-oriented care are a matter of course and still part of the airline's "heart and soul" – even though times have changed and only several hours' flying time separate New York's Fifth Avenue from Zurich's Bahnhofstrasse. Life has become faster, more intense and livelier in the meantime, and hopping from one world to another has become easier. Some things about Swissair have changed over the years, too. It has also become faster, better and livelier.

Rolf von Siebenthal, Gate Gourmet Zurich, Ltd. Chef/Head of Product Development. Born in Winterthur, Switzerland in 1943, Rolf von Siebenthal decided to work in Swissair's airline catering division after having completed his training as a cook and gaining a few years of experience. He learned the new profession by starting at the bottom and working his way up – and is today responsible for the quality of 33,000 meals a day and for all new culinary developments in the test kitchen. Over the decades, with his own thoroughness, Rolf von Siebenthal has acquired a profound knowledge of the prevailing food and kitchen technologies and culinary trends. Rolf von Siebenthal was the driving force behind and major influence on all of Swissair's new catering concepts. His immense know-how and his pragmatism were decisive in the successful introduction of the natural**gourmet** line on board.

The culinary foundation at 37,000 feet
is provided at ground level
by Rolf von Siebenthal,
Gate Gourmet Zurich, Ltd.
Chef/Head of Product Development

Rolf v. Siebenthal

A High-Flying Chef with Both Feet on the Ground

The introduction of natural**gourmet** was also a challenge for test cooks Silvio Bigger and Walter Alfare – together with Rolf von Siebenthal, they transformed a great idea into reality!

If I had not become a cook, I would have ...

... become a cook anyway.

My most important milestones in the history of Swissair catering were ...

... the Marco Polo buffets on the Far East route, the menus created by Michelin chefs – including those by Fredy Girardet for First Class. A major step forward in the history of catering was the dawn of the jumbo jet era – suddenly there were 370 instead of 150 people to feed on each plane!

And at the end of the eighties, when Swissair became the first airline to produce an environmental audit, this of course had a major influence on the whole catering concept. It began with the purchase of ingredients and led right on through to recycling. For me, the introduction of natural**gourmet** was a logical and consistent extension of the environmentally conscious basic idea. It was a big challenge for me and for the whole team – and I'm pretty sure it won't be the last one.

A difficult situation that I remember ...

... There are many. Whether in catering, on a club vacation or in the mountains when the weather suddenly changes – sound decisions are often needed.

The most important thing to me about my profession is ...

... quality. Thinking things through. No superficiality. That also means being persistent. And maybe even a bit unpleasant at times.

Besides my profession ...

... there is the Kloten ice hockey team, my dog Jess, the famous pile of trade papers, my friends, and of course my family.

For me, holidays mean ...

... carefree days in the most remote mountain valleys of Switzerland, in Santa Maria – where I can enjoy the mountains, nature, unspoiled surroundings, the down-home hospitality of the locals, a slower pace, different values, different feelings – just another kind of pleasure.

Pet peeves, strange habits and passions? ...

... Whew! Well, let's keep it harmless: One of my passions is the mountains. And the pet peeves? Do I have to answer that? [Editor's note: No!]

If my wife would describe me, she would say that I am ...

... stable, reliable, persistent and sometimes too realistic, because everything has to make sense for me. The rest I'm not telling.

If I were stranded on the legendary desert island, I would like to have with me ...

... My wife and my dog.

Why? ...

... Because I couldn't leave one of them behind without spoiling the relationship with the other.

My last word ...

... I don't like interviews.

Smoked Trout on Pumpernickel Rounds

4 small slices pumpernickel
butter
fresh, grated horseradish
4 small lettuce leaves
4 small pieces smoked trout fillet
4 small sprigs dill

1 Using a scone or biscuit cutter, stamp out pieces of pumpernickel into the desired shapes about 2½cm in diameter. Mix the butter with a little grated horseradish and spread the pumpernickel with it. Put a lettuce leaf on top, cover with a piece of trout and garnish with dill.

Greetings from the Kitchen

Air-Dried Beef and Cheese Rolls

4 slices air-dried beef, not too thinly sliced
4 slices Gruyère, thinly sliced, about the same size as the beef
cream cheese

1 Place a slice of Gruyère on top of each slice of air-dried beef, spread with cream cheese, roll up and cut the ends on a slight slant.

Dates with Cream Cheese

4 dates
50g cream cheese

1 Halve and stone the dates. Stuff with cream cheese using a forcing bag with star-shaped nozzle.

Terrine of Leek, Sea Trout and Pike-Perch with a Herby Tomato Vinaigrette

For a 25cm loaf tin or terrine

400g small pike-perch fillets
400g small sea trout fillets
juice of 2 lemons
100g butter
500ml fish stock (see recipe page 192)
50g aspic jelly crystals
2 tbsp dry white vermouth
500g baby leeks, trimmed but green part left on
salt and freshly ground pepper

150ml herby tomato vinaigrette
(see recipe page 191)

1 Season the fish fillets and sprinkle with the lemon juice. Fry gently in the hot butter until just done, drain on paper towels and cool.

2 Dissolve the aspic jelly crystals in the hot stock, add the vermouth and cool.

3 Blanch the leeks in boiling salted water, drain and plunge immediately in cold water to set

the colour. Drain again and pat dry on paper towels. Split the leeks in half lengthwise and separate the leaves. Season. Drape the leek leaves in the terrine so that the bottom and sides are covered. Make a double layer in the bottom. Fill the terrine with successive layers of sea trout, pike-perch and leeks, adding a little jelly each time. Finish with a double layer of leeks, add the rest of the jelly and chill for 24 hours.

4 Slice the terrine and arrange on plates. Drizzle a little vinaigrette over the corner of each slice.

Ceps in a Cream Sauce with Poached Pears

2 small pears, stalks left on, preferably a green-skinned variety
2 tbsp lemon juice
½ litre water
50g caster sugar

200g ceps
50g butter
1 shallot, finely chopped
100ml white wine
3 tbsp dark veal stock (see recipe, page 192)
a little paprika
½ litre whipping cream
salt and freshly ground pepper

a little butter
1 tbsp caster sugar

1 Peel the pears, halve them (if possible leaving a piece of stem attached) and remove the cores. Sprinkle with a little of the lemon juice. Put the water, sugar and remaining lemon juice in a pan and poach the pears gently until barely cooked.

2 Cut the ceps in thick, even slices, season and fry them briefly in some of the butter. Keep them warm. Soften the shallot in the rest of the butter, moisten with the wine and veal glaze, add the paprika and cream and cook steadily until reduced to about 350ml. Taste for seasoning, adjusting if necessary.

3 Drain and dry the pears on paper towels. Melt the butter and sugar together and cook to a caramel. Turn the pears carefully in the caramel.

4 Arrange the ceps on heated plates, pour over the sauce and garnish with the pears.

A **melon baller** is a small sharp-edged, half moon-shaped spoon used to scoop out rounds of melon, potatoes or other vegetable

34

200g fillet of veal
1 litre light veal stock (see recipe page 192)
1 leek, white part only
1 piece of celeriac
½ onion

1 tbsp honey
3 tbsp herb vinegar
6 tbsp safflower oil
salt and freshly ground pepper

about 24 small yellow melon balls (e.g. Charentais)
about 20 small green melon balls (e.g. Ogen or honeydew)
about 16 cherry tomatoes

Poached Veal and Melon Salad

1 Tie the veal to a wooden spoon so that it keeps its shape. Poach it in the veal stock with the leek, celeriac and onion for about 10 minutes depending on thickness until just cooked but still pink in the middle (a meat thermometer should read about 60°C). Let it cool in the stock.

2 Dissolve the honey in the warm vinegar, add the oil, season to taste.

3 Cut the meat in paper-thin (1mm) slices, arrange on plates with the melon balls and cherry tomatoes and sprinkle the dressing over.

Herbed and Crumb-Crusted Chops

1 small shallot, finely chopped

1 clove garlic, mashed

25g butter

a little parsley, chopped

marjoram, thyme, oregano and basil, finely chopped

2 tbsp fresh white breadcrumbs (from a sliced white loaf, crusts removed)

salt and freshly ground pepper

4 well trimmed lamb chops, each about 50g

butter for frying

1 For the crumb crust, soften the shallot and garlic in the butter. Add the herbs and cook a little longer. Stir in the breadcrumbs, mix well.

2 Heat the oven to 200ºC/Gas 6. Season the chops and sear them very briefly in a frying pan in a little butter. They should remain pink inside. Spread them with the herby crumbs, pressing down well. Roast them in the top of the oven (if possible with good top heat) until a crust forms.

Duo of Lamb Chops

Cream of Carrot Soup

1 shallot, finely chopped
1 leek, white part only, sliced
300g carrots, peeled and sliced
25g butter
1 tsp curry powder
400ml light veal or chicken stock
(see recipe page 192)
300ml + 4 tbsp whipping cream
salt and freshly ground pepper

12 carrot balls, cut with a melon baller,
blanched
chives

Strudel-Wrapped Chops

50g mushrooms, finely chopped
15g butter
2 tbsp whipping cream
4 mint leaves, snipped
salt and freshly ground pepper
4 well trimmed lamb chops, each
about 50g
olive oil
125g strudel pastry (see recipe page 193)
1 egg to glaze
15g melted butter

1 Sweat the mushrooms briefly in the butter, add the cream, cook down a bit, stir in the snipped mint leaves and season to taste. Season the chops, sear them briefly in hot oil and let them cool. When cool, spread the mushroom mixture on top of the chops.

2 Heat the oven to 200ºC/Gas 6. Roll out the strudel pastry very thinly and cut into 15cm circles. Wrap the chops in the pastry, leaving the ends of the bones exposed (these can be topped with a cutlet frill after baking). Brush the pastry with egg and bake the chops for about 6 minutes. Remove from the oven and brush with melted butter. Slip cutlet frills onto the exposed bones. Serve both sorts of chops on heated plates with a rich lamb stock (see recipe page 192).

1 Soften the shallot, leek and carrots in the butter. Sprinkle with curry powder, moisten with the stock and simmer till the vegetables are soft.

2 Blend till smooth in the liquidiser or food processor, strain, add 300ml of the cream, bring back to a boil and season to taste.

3 Divide the soup between heated soup bowls, stir in the reserved cream, garnish with 2–3 carrot balls and some chives.

To blanch means to bring delicate foods (e.g. vegetables, fruit, sweetbreads etc.) briefly to a boil, or to immerse them briefly in boiling water, in order to slightly pre-cook them.

Grilled Rabbit Legs with Mustard Sauce

4 hind legs of rabbit, each about 100g
extra-virgin olive oil
salt and freshly ground pepper

100ml light veal stock
(see recipe page 192)
2 tbsp white wine
1 tbsp coarse grain mustard
½ tbsp mild Dijon mustard
150ml whipping cream

1 Put the stock, wine and mustard in a pan and bring to a boil. Add the cream and cook steadily to reduce to about 150ml. Season to taste.

2 Heat the oven to 150°C/Gas 2. Season the rabbit legs and sear in hot oil on both sides. Finish off in the oven for about 10 minutes or until just done. Serve with the sauce.

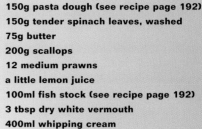

Shellfish Lasagne

150g pasta dough (see recipe page 192)
150g tender spinach leaves, washed
75g butter
200g scallops
12 medium prawns
a little lemon juice
100ml fish stock (see recipe page 192)
3 tbsp dry white vermouth
400ml whipping cream
salt and freshly ground pepper
nutmeg

25g grated Parmesan

1 Roll out the pasta dough thinly and cut 12 lasagne rounds each about 9cm in diameter. Cook gently in simmering salted water for about 2 minutes. Lift out and drain them, then leave in a bowl of cold water so that they do not stick together.

2 Stew the spinach leaves for a few minutes in 25g of the butter with salt, pepper and a little nutmeg.

3 Slice the scallops ½cm thick, cut the prawns in half lengthwise. Season both with salt, pepper and a little lemon juice and fry briefly in the rest of the butter.

4 Boil the fish stock and vermouth hard to reduce by half. Add the cream, reduce again to about 250ml. Check the seasoning, adjusting if necessary.

5 Butter some individual ovenproof gratin dishes. Put some spinach in the bottom, cover with a lasagne round, top with scallops and some sauce. Add another lasagne round, prawns and more sauce. Finish with a lasagne round and the rest of the sauce, and sprinkle with Parmesan.

6 Heat the oven to 250ºC/Gas 9. Bake the lasagnes briefly until thoroughly hot and the tops nicely golden-brown.

Pizarro Potato Pie

For an 18cm-diameter quiche tin

400g potatoes
1 shallot, finely chopped
25g butter
a little marjoram, finely chopped
150ml whipping cream
salt and freshly ground pepper

250g shortcrust pastry
(see recipe page 193)
egg yolk to glaze

1 Peel the potatoes and slice them thinly. Soften the shallot in the butter, add the potatoes, marjoram and cream and season to taste. Simmer very gently so that the potatoes do not fall apart. Stop the cooking before they are quite tender (they should retain a bit of bite), remove from the heat and allow them to cool.

2 Cut the pastry in two pieces, one slightly larger than the other. Butter the tin. Roll out the larger piece to a circle slightly larger than the tin and lay it in, leaving about a 1cm-overhang all around. Spoon in the cooled potatoes. Turn the pastry edge in over the potatoes and brush it with egg yolk. Roll out the second piece a bit smaller and lay it on top of the potatoes to form a lid. Press the edges together well to seal. Brush the top with more egg yolk and make a steam hole in the middle. Leave in a cool place for about an hour.

3 Heat the oven to 200ºC/Gas 6. Bake the pie for 25–30 minutes.

Vegetable Feuilletés with a Creamy Herb Sauce

125g puff pastry
egg yolk to glaze

4 medium thick green asparagus spears, the lower part peeled
4 medium thick white asparagus spears, peeled
15g butter
a pinch of sugar
a quarter each of green, red and yellow pepper
150ml asparagus cooking water
3 tbsp dry white vermouth
600ml whipping cream
a little thyme, oregano, basil and parsley, finely chopped
salt and freshly ground pepper

1 Heat the oven to 200ºC/Gas 6. Roll out the pastry to a rectangle of about 30x15cm, 2mm thick. Trim all the edges and cut in 4 rectangles. Prick with a fork, brush with egg yolk and allow to rest for a few minutes. Bake for 10–15 minutes until golden brown.

2 Cook the asparagus spears in boiling salted water with the butter and a pinch of sugar until just tender. Drain, reserving the cooking water. Cut 5cm lengths off the top and reserve these tips for the garnish. Cut the rest in 4cm pieces.

3 Roast or grill the pepper quarters until thoroughly blackened, rub off the skin and cut the flesh in large, even, lozenge-shaped pieces.

4 Put 150ml of the reserved asparagus cooking water in a pan with the vermouth, boil down hard to reduce by half, add the cream and reduce again to about 400ml. Add the reserved asparagus pieces, the pepper lozenges and a little of the finely chopped herbs to the sauce, season to taste.

5 Split the puff pastry cases in half horizontally, spoon some filling and sauce onto the pastry base and arrange the tips so that they stick out a bit. Put the tops on and surround with more filling.

Strips of orange or lemon **zest** can be obtained with the help of a zester, or by using a potato peeler and cutting the zest into fine strips. It is important only to use the outer layer of the peel, without the bitter white part.

Semolina Strudel with Sultanas and an Apricot Sauce

125ml milk
25g brown sugar
a pinch of salt
25g semolina
grated zest of ½ a lemon
1 egg yolk
1 tbsp whipping cream
1 tsp quark or *fromage frais*
50g sultanas

125g strudel pastry (see recipe page 193)
25g butter, melted

500g fresh or frozen apricots, halved, stoned and finely diced
150g brown sugar
1–2 tbsp lemon juice

1 Bring the milk to a boil with the sugar and salt. Add the semolina and lemon zest and cook over gentle heat, stirring, till the semolina is soft. Mix in the egg yolk, cream, quark or *fromage frais* and sultanas, bring back to the boil and allow to cool.

2 Form the cooled semolina into a bolster shape. Roll out the strudel pastry very thinly and wrap the semolina in it. Brush with some of the melted butter and prick several times with a fork.

3 Cook the apricot pieces with the sugar and lemon juice until just soft, blend to a smooth purée in the liquidiser or food processor. Push them through a sieve.

4 Heat the oven to 250ºC/Gas 9. Bake the strudel for 15–20 minutes until golden brown. Remove and brush again with melted butter. Reheat the apricot sauce briefly and spoon some onto each plate. Cut the strudel carefully into thick slices and place a slice on top of the sauce. Garnish as wished.

Natural Gourmet

There is a new MILKY WAY

It leads from a tiny little piece of land up to an altitude of at least

37,000 feet, and goes all around the world. Although this phenomenon is

not even visible with the most powerful telescope, Swissair passengers have

the pleasure of eating and drinking from it: the cream in the coffee or the

milk in the dessert comes from Berta, who loves to gaze at the Alpine

panorama as she chews her cud. Or from Olga, who has the most beautiful

horns far and wide. Or from Rita, Susi, Trudi, Blüemli, Vreni, Züsi or

however they are called.

It wasn't easy.

At the time, NATURAL-GOURMET was seeking 1.6 millions litres of organic milk per year. And they needed it right away. That pretty much exceeded everyone's capacity, even that of the large Swiss milk industry. Falling back on foreign markets was not an option for environmental reasons because of the long transportation routes.

WHEN IT FINALLY COME, the solution was easy. Its name was Markus Forster, came from Canton Appenzell, and confirmed the legend of the shrewd hill people.

Heidi and Markus Forster

AS THE OWNER OF A SMALL CHEESE DAIRY, Markus Forster quickly recognised the chance for his operation and for organic farming in general – and quickly acted on it. He was able to convince and win over almost all the organic farmers in the region for the NATURAL**GOURMET** idea. Today, he and his fellow farmers deliver over 4000 litres of fresh organic milk to the diary, where – under strictly controlled conditions – it is processed into butter, sour cream and sweet cream. While Markus Forster was laughed at a few years ago as a fool for championing the cause of organic products, many now envy his secure source of income. That he, as a small-scale dairy-man, beat out the large dairies, pleases Markus Forster. "Sometimes there are advantages to being small," grins the tall Appenzeller. "I didn't have to write any clever strategy statements, convince any board of directors or otherwise consult any supervisors. I asked my wife. And she has a quick mind." The Forsters were able to double their turnover in one move. The staff was increased from 9 to 13 people. It didn't take any more than that, and if it became necessary, both sons also pitched in at the filling machines.

THE MILKY WAY FROM IDYLLIC APPENZELL UP TO AN ALTITUDE 37,000 FEET HAS BEEN ESTABLISHED. *The present delivery commitment is great, and demand from other sources is also increasing. So Markus Forster is continuing to try to win over other farmers in the area for organic farming, because he doesn't want to have to buy milk from the larger dairies in the lowlands. "This 'milk tourism' is unnecessary and just the opposite of environmentally sound." Nevertheless, Markus Forster doesn't put just any farmer under contract. He is choosy; he wants to check out the farm and its livestock himself, to talk to the farmers – and he wants to have a good feeling about the whole thing. Because all the inspections and tests cannot replace the personal trust that is the real deciding factor for Markus Forster. And every time he is collecting milk from the farms at the break of dawn, he knows that he has put his Milky Way into the right hands. That this very special Milky Way was only possible because of him and each and every organic farmer who works with him. Sometimes, when the early morning sky is brightening over the hills of Appenzell, if he looks carefully, he can see a long, narrow trail of white in the sky on the horizon. Then his face breaks into a contented smile. Forster is a happy man.*

There once was a chicken, a cannibal, too

Who one evening had nothing to do

She considered not a lot,

and threw all her eggs in a pot

Choked back a tear, and hoped that no one was near

Ate all the eggs up and enjoyed every bite

And thus invented scrambled eggs that night!

AND YET ANOTHER APPENZELLER LOVE STORY. *This one is about the spring wind, the summer heat, the rich mildness of fall, and about the time of maturing and resting. It is a love story about hops and malt and about a small brewery in Appenzell that is still brewing the golden juice of the barley according to the purity requirements from the year 1516. Which would not be so unusual if it had not been for the vision of an organic beer. Today, brewmaster Karl Locher is proud of his organic beer, the first of its kind in Switzerland: "Beer is a beverage that is created from life – the pure spring water of the Alps brings with it the memory of the path it has followed through the layers of rock; hops and malt carry the song of summer and the bees in them, and the yeast and the brewmaster's loving touch initiate the fermentation process. The living process begins." In the stone cellar, what will later become "Naturperle" (the pearl of nature) is maturing: a beer with its own character, just as nature made it.*

Boiled Beef Salad with Herby Champagne Dressing

Recipe by Roland Jöhri

Herby Champagne Dressing:
100ml Champagne vinegar
1 tbsp finely chopped gherkins
1 tbsp chopped flat-leaved parsley
1 tbsp chopped mixed herbs (e.g. chervil, dill, basil)
4–5 capers, chopped
coarse salt and freshly ground pepper

1 red pepper
1 green and 1 yellow courgette
4 mini sweetcorns
4 slices aubergine
4 slices ceps or shiitake mushrooms
olive oil
Balsamic vinegar
500g boiled beef, well marbled with fat

1 Mix together all the ingredients for the Champagne dressing except the herbs (which should only be added at the end, otherwise they will discolour). Taste for seasoning.

2 For the salad, cut the vegetables in nice, medium-sized pieces, brush with oil and season. Put them under a hot grill, or toss in a pan over moderate heat until soft. Sprinkle with the vinegar and leave to marinate.

3 Slice the boiled beef thinly and divide it between the plates. Add the herbs to the dressing. Arrange the vegetables in the middle of the plate and sprinkle the beef generously with the dressing.

Calf's Head with a Herby Tomato Vinaigrette

Recipe by Rolf von Siebenthal

800g calf's head
2 litres light veal stock (see recipe page 192)
juice of ½ a lemon
2 tbsp white wine vinegar
1 leek, white part only
a piece of celeriac
½ onion, peeled
salt
a bouquet garni (thyme, rosemary, marjoram, bay leaf)
1 tsp peppercorns, crushed

150ml herby tomato vinaigrette (see recipe page 191)

1 Blanch the calf's head, rinse under running water, leave to dry a bit. Trim well, taking care to remove the rough mouth lining, any excess fat and any dark spots or hairs.

2 Bring the stock to a boil, add the calf's head, the wine, lemon juice, vinegar, vegetables, bouquet garni, peppercorns and salt to taste. Simmer gently, skimming occasionally, for about 20 minutes until tender.

3 Slice the calf's head thinly and sprinkle with the vinaigrette.

Pearl Barley Soup from the Grisons

Recipe by Roland Jöhri

150g onions
150g leeks
100g carrots
50g celeriac
75g raw ham
75g air-dried beef
25g butter
100g pearl barley
50g dried white beans
3 litres chicken stock
300ml whipping cream
3 egg yolks
salt and freshly ground pepper

Tip: Smoked pork or bacon can also be cooked with the soup. In this case, take care with the seasoning.

1 Chop the onions, and cut the leeks, carrots, celeriac, ham and beef in small cubes. Sweat them all together in the butter, add the pearl barley and cook a little more. Season to taste. Add the beans and the stock and simmer the soup for about 1½ hours.

2 Remove the soup from the heat and stir in the cream and the egg yolks to thicken. Check the seasoning, adjusting if necessary.

Sparkling Sauerkraut Soup with Caraway

Recipe by Wolfgang Kuchler

50g shallots, finely sliced
½ an apple, peeled and sliced
1 tbsp caraway seeds
25g butter
200ml dry Champagne
200g cooked sauerkraut, finely chopped
½ litre light veal stock (see recipe page 192)
100ml double cream
white Balsamic vinegar
salt and freshly ground pepper
a pinch of sugar
olive oil

1 Soften the shallots and apple in the butter with the caraway seeds without allowing them to brown. Moisten with the Champagne and cook till this has almost completely evaporated. Add the sauerkraut and cook together briefly before adding the stock. Cover and simmer together gently for about 30 minutes.

2 Whisk in the enrichment cream and a splash of vinegar. Boil up again briefly and season to taste. Blend till smooth in a liquidiser and strain. Serve sprinkled with a little olive oil.

Apple Salad with Smoked Duck Breast

Recipe by Rolf von Siebenthal

1 tbsp raisins
300g red apples, quartered and cored
3 tbsp lemon juice
200ml water
2 tbsp honey
4 tbsp whipping cream
pepper

16 slices smoked duck breast, sliced
lengthwise

1 Soak the raisins briefly in warm water. Slice the apples and sprinkle with 2 tablespoons of lemon juice to prevent discolouring.

2 Dissolve the honey in the remaining lemon juice in a small pan. Lift the apple slices out of their lemon juice, pat them dry with paper towels and add them to the pan. Drain the raisins, season with a little pepper. Whip the cream till it forms soft peaks and stir it in also.

3 Divide the apple salad evenly between four plates and arrange four duck slices on top of each portion.

Tip:
Do not prepare the salad too far in advance, it is best done just before serving.

Poached Chicken in a White Sauce

Recipe by Rolf von Siebenthal

2 spring chickens (poussins), each about 450g

a piece of onion, celeriac and leek

1 bay leaf

5 peppercorns

salt

Sauce:

150ml chicken stock (from cooking the chickens)

400ml whipping cream

3 tbsp sparkling white wine

salt and freshly ground pepper

a little lemon juice, optional

Worcester sauce

Garnish:

a little carrot, cut in matchstick strips

a little leek, green part only, cut in matchstick strips

a suspicion of truffle, cut in thin strips, optional

Tip:
Serve this dish with plainly boiled rice.

Fillet of Pike-Perch Farmhouse-Style

Recipe by Cuno Blattner

4 fillets of pike-perch, each about 100g
1 tbsp extra-virgin olive oil
2 tbsp whipping cream
250g potatoes
25g butter
1 courgette, cut in cubes
1 carrot, cut in cubes
2 tomatoes, skinned, seeded and cut in cubes
juice of 1 lemon
100ml whipping cream
1 tbsp finely chopped parsley
1 tbsp finely chopped chives
2 tbsp brown veal glaze
salt and freshly ground pepper

1 Season the fish fillets. Mix together the olive oil and cream, spread it on the fillets and leave to marinate. Peel the potato, cut in cubes, blanch and drain them well. Fry till golden brown in some of the butter. Cook the courgette and carrot in boiling salted water until barely tender.

2 Fry the fish briefly in the rest of the butter until golden brown, turning once. Lift onto heated plates. Sweat the tomato cubes gently in the same pan, add the courgette and carrot cubes, season to taste and stir in the lemon juice, cream, parsley and chives. Heat the veal glaze. Spoon the vegetables over the fish and sprinkle with a little veal glaze. Scatter the fried potatoes on top.

1 Cover the chickens with cold water and bring to a boil. Drain and rinse under cold running water. Put the vegetables, bay leaf, peppercorns and salt in the pan, add water and bring to a boil. Put in the chickens and simmer gently for about 40 minutes. Lift out and keep them warm. Strain the stock through a muslin.

2 Measure out 150ml of the stock (the rest can be used for risotto or soup) and put it in a pan with the cream and wine. Bring to a boil and simmer for a few minutes. Season to taste, sharpen if wished with a little lemon juice and a add a couple of splashes of Worcester sauce.

3 For the garnish, blanch the vegetables in a little of the chicken stock. Toss the truffle strips (if used) in a little hot butter. Cut the chickens in half and remove all bones except the wing bones. Put a leg and a piece of breast on each plate and pour the sauce over. Scatter the vegetable and truffle garnish on top and serve.

Granny's Veal Loaf with Mashed Potatoes

Recipe by Rolf von Siebenthal

Mashed Potatoes

400g potatoes, peeled
25g butter
100ml hot milk
3 tbsp whipping cream
salt and freshly ground pepper
nutmeg

1 Cut the potatoes in even-sized pieces and cook them in boiling salted water. Drain, leave them in the colander to let off steam a bit, then mash them.

2 Add the butter, milk and cream to the mashed potatoes. Beat till smooth. Season to taste with salt, pepper and nutmeg.

For a medium-sized loaf tin

50g white bread, crusts removed
5 tbsp warm milk
25g shallots, chopped
25g butter
a little marjoram, oregano and thyme,
finely chopped
400g not too lean minced veal
1 egg
salt and freshly ground pepper
oil for the tin

Sauce:
3 tbsp red wine
1 shallot, chopped
400ml dark veal stock (see recipe
page 192)
a small piece of celeriac and carrot,
finely chopped

1 Soak the bread in the milk. Soften the shallots in the butter, add the herbs, mix with the soaked bread and leave to stand for an hour.

2 Heat the oven to 200ºC/Gas 6. Add the bread mixture to the minced meat with the egg, beating to mix well. Season to taste. Form into a loaf shape. Brush out the loaf tin with a little oil and press the meat loaf into it. Bake for 20–30 minutes.

3 For the sauce, simmer the wine with the shallot, add the veal stock and boil down to reduce to about 300ml. Add the cubed vegetables, bring back to the boil and season to taste.

4 duck breasts
1 tbsp peanut oil
50g black olives
1 tbsp olive oil
2 sprigs thyme
salt and freshly ground pepper

Mignonette Potatoes:
600g large potatoes
2 tbsp oil
25g butter
nutmeg

1 Heat the oven to 180°C/Gas 4. Slash
the skin of the duck breasts with a sharp knife to
give a nice crust. Sear them on both sides in the hot
peanut oil, then finish the cooking, skin side down,
in the oven for 12 minutes. Leave them aside for a
while to let the meat rest a little.

2 For the mignonette potatoes, peel the
potatoes and cut in sticks about ½cm thick and
4cm long. Soak in cold water for 15 minutes, lift
out and drain them. Pat dry with a tea-towel. Heat
some oil in a frying pan and fry the potato sticks.
Finish them off in a 200°C/Gas 6 oven until golden
brown, turning them occasionally. Drain off the fat,
add the butter and finish cooking the potatoes in it.
Season with salt, pepper and nutmeg.

3 Heat the olives gently in the olive oil
with the thyme sprigs. Cut the duck in slices and
splay them out. Serve with the warm olives.

Duck Breast with Olives and Mignonette Potatoes

Recipe by Roland Jöhri

Veal Pojarski with Creamy Mushroom Sauce

Recipe by Roland Jöhri

600g trimmed lean roast of veal
150g white bread, cut in small cubes
3 tbsp milk
1 large shallot, chopped
a knob of butter
200ml whipping cream
a bunch of parsley, chopped
a little rosemary and thyme
breadcrumbs
50g melted butter
salt and freshly ground pepper

Creamy mushroom sauce:
15g dried or 50g fresh ceps
1 tsp finely chopped shallot
a knob of butter
2 tsp Cognac
2 tsp Madeira
3 tbsp dry white wine
5 tbsp chicken or veal stock (see recipe page 192)
3 tbsp veal stock, reduced to
1 tbsp syrupy *jus*
100ml whipping cream + a little to decorate
15g chilled butter

1 Mince the meat using the finest blade of the mincer or process finely in a food processor. Soak the bread cubes in the milk. Soften the shallot in the butter, allow to cool.

2 Set a mixing bowl over ice cubes and put the minced meat in it. Work in the cream gradually, season and mix in the bread, shallot, parsley, rosemary and thyme bit by bit. Form the mixture into 'cutlets', two per person. Coat with breadcrumbs and fry gently in the butter.

3 For the sauce, soak the dried mushrooms in warm water until soft. Rinse two or three times, squeeze them out. Cut them in half lengthwise, and in half again if necessary. (Slice the fresh mushrooms in the same way, if using.)

4 Soften the shallot in a little butter, add the mushrooms and cook briefly together. Pour in the Cognac and set it alight. (If fresh mushrooms are used, these should be removed from the pan at this stage, otherwise they will be overcooked.) Add the Madeira and white wine and simmer together gently. Add the stock, the reduced *jus* and the cream and cook to a coating consistency. Remove the mushrooms, whisk in the chilled butter and season to taste. Replace the mushrooms in the sauce and fold in a little whipped cream to enrich.

Braised Duck in a Rosemary Sauce with Polenta

Recipe by Wolfgang Kuchler

1 Nantes or Challans duck, oven-ready, about 2kg

salt and freshly ground pepper

plain white flour

clarified butter or a mixture of butter and oil

25g butter

1 tbsp olive oil

200g mixed vegetables, diced fine (carrots, celeriac, onions)

a large sprig of rosemary

1 tbsp tomato purée

1 bottle red wine

500ml veal or chicken stock

Polenta:

300ml milk

350ml chicken stock

125g coarsely ground polenta flour

olive oil

grated Parmesan

1 Cut the duck in four pieces and toss in seasoned flour. Brown on all sides in the clarified butter (or butter and oil), remove from the pan and keep them warm. Tip away the fat, add half of the

remaining butter and the olive oil. Soften the vegetables in it with the rosemary. Stir in the tomato purée and sprinkle on a little flour. Moisten with the wine and add the stock.

2 Heat the oven to 200ºC/Gas 6. Put the duck pieces back in the pan, cover and braise gently for about 1½ hours. Lift the duck pieces out of the pan, strain the sauce and if necessary cook down a little to reduce. Put the duck pieces back into the reduced sauce.

3 For the polenta, put the milk, stock and polenta in a saucepan with olive oil and salt to taste. Bring slowly to a boil, stirring, and simmer gently until thickened. It should be fairly soft. Shortly before serving stir in the Parmesan and the rest of the butter.

1 For the filling, season the veal with salt and pepper. Soak the bread in the milk. Heat the butter and stew the meat gently in it with the bread and shallots. Mince everything finely together in a mincer or food processor. Put the minced meat in a bowl over ice cubes and gradually work in the cream. Season to taste.

2 Season the beef and lay a slice of bacon on top of each slice. Divide the filling between them and roll them up to form paupiettes. Fix with toothpicks. Brown them on all sides in the hot oil. Drain off the fat and deglaze the pan with the red wine. Cook down hard to reduce to a quarter of its volume, then add the veal stock. Poach the paupiettes gently in the liquid, basting regularly, then remove and keep them warm. Cook the sauce down a bit more, taste for seasoning. Finally, whisk in the chilled butter. Do not allow the sauce to boil again.

3 Arrange the paupiettes on plates and pour the sauce over.

Beef Paupiettes with Pinot Noir

Recipe by Roland Jöhri

Filling:

100g stewing veal

25g white bread, cut in cubes

2 tbsp milk

1 tbsp finely chopped shallots

15g butter

3 tbsp whipping cream

salt and freshly ground pepper

8 slices of rump or entrecote steak, each about 50g, thinly sliced and beaten out flat

8 thin slices streaky bacon

2 tbsp peanut oil

300ml red wine (e.g. Pinot Noir)

200ml well reduced veal stock (see recipe page 192)

25g chilled butter, cut in pieces

Tip:
Mushrooms make a good accompaniment, along with mashed potatoes or gnocchi.

450g beef, well trimmed
250g potatoes
salt and freshly ground pepper, nutmeg
a sprig of marjoram, leaves stripped off
100g sausage casings (natural or artificial)

For the dried beans:
200g dried green (French) beans, brought
to a boil and soaked overnight in the
cooking water
1 onion, chopped
50g smoked lean bacon, cut in small cubes
50g butter
200ml vegetable stock

Beef and Potato Sausages with Marjoram and Dried Beans

Recipe by Roland Jöhri

1 Mince or process the beef coarsely in a mincer or food processor. Peel the potatoes, dice them small and cook until barely tender. Add them to the minced beef, season with salt, pepper, nutmeg and marjoram and mix thoroughly together. Fill into the sausage casings. Take care not to fill them too tightly and leave no air pockets. Tie in four equal lengths with kitchen string. Poach the sausages gently in lightly salted water for 15 minutes.

2 Drain the soaked beans well. Soften the onion and bacon in the butter. Add the beans and cook a little longer. Moisten with the vegetable stock, season to taste and cook gently for 1½ hours or until tender. Taste to see.

**Tip:
Apple sauce
goes beauti-
fully with
these sau-
sages.**

Creamy Leeks with
Tomato Strips
Recipe by Rolf von Siebenthal

200g leeks, trimmed
15g butter
150ml whipping cream
**2 tomatoes, skinned, seeded, halved and
cut in strips**
salt and freshly ground pepper

1 Cut the leeks in matchstick strips.
Blanch, drain and refresh in cold water. Drain well
and pat them dry. Cook them briefly in the hot
butter, add the cream and bubble up together to a
creamy sauce. Do not overcook. Just before serving,
mix in the tomato strips, and check the seasoning,
adjusting if necessary.

**Rye Bread
from
Poschiavo
and Pear
Bread from
the Grisons
(see basic
recipes
pages 190
and 191)**

Dried Apricot and Brioche Pudding with Caramel Ice Cream

Recipe by Wolfgang Kuchler

For a medium-sized soufflé dish

125g brioche
50g butter, melted and cooled
50g dried apricots, cut in cubes
100ml milk
100ml whipping cream
1 vanilla pod, split, seeds scraped out
1 egg
2 tbsp caster sugar
50g apricot jam, sieved
Grand Marnier
4 tbsp caramel or vanilla ice cream
mint leaves, optional

1 Heat the oven to 120ºC/Gas ½. Butter the soufflé dish. Slice the brioche, brush the slices with butter and arrange them in layers in the dish. Sprinkle with the apricot pieces. In a saucepan heat together the milk, cream and vanilla seeds. Whisk in the egg and sugar and pour this mixture over the brioche. Place the dish in a roasting pan, pour in boiling water to come halfway up the sides. Bake for 20–30 minutes or until set.

2 Mix the apricot jam with some Grand Marnier in a little pan and heat it gently. Brush it over the top of the pudding. Cut in portions and serve with a scoop of ice cream. If wished, decorate with mint leaves.

Lebkuchen Spice Mousse

Recipe by Rolf von Siebenthal

75g dark chocolate or couverture
1 egg yolk
2 tbsp brown sugar
2 tbsp rum
2 tsp *Lebkuchen* spice*
250ml whipping cream

4 slices kiwi
a few raspberries
a little grated chocolate

1 Break up the chocolate and put it in a bowl over barely simmering water with the egg yolk, sugar, rum and spice. Heat until melted. Whip the cream and fold it into the cooled chocolate mixture. Pour into a glass bowl and chill for a few hours.

2 Spoon out nice ovals of the mousse using a soup spoon dipped in hot water. Serve 3 per plate, garnish with the kiwi and the raspberries and sprinkle grated chocolate on top.

*Lebkuchen spice is a special mixture of ground aniseed, cloves, coriander, nutmeg, pepper and cinnamon.

Couverture is a special confectioner's chocolate with a high cocoa buttercontent, especially good for coating baked goods etc.

Rhubarb Soufflés

Recipe by Roland Jöhri

For 4 ramekins

75g rhubarb
100ml milk
2 eggs, separated + 1 egg white
1 tbsp low-fat quark or *fromage frais*
25g butter, melted
75g bread cubes
2 tbsp ground almonds
2 tbsp caster sugar
lemon zest
butter for the ramekins

1 Trim and peel the rhubarb, cut in cubes and cook briefly in boiling water. Drain.

2 Heat the milk gently, stir in the egg yolks. Pour this mixture over the bread cubes, add the quark or *fromage frais*, the ground almonds and the melted butter. Mix in the rhubarb cubes, sugar and lemon zest.

3 Beat the egg whites until stiff and fold them in gently. Tip the mixture into the buttered ramekins and bake them in a bain-marie at 170ºC/Gas 3 for 35–40 minutes. Turn them out and sprinkle with icing sugar.

"A common table brings people together, which is why a shared meal has become an important instrument in politics and in understanding..."

Antoine Marie Carême

Food and power, the power of food.

The fact that Talleyrand, the earl and wizard of French diplomacy, is said to have handled the famous chef Carême with kid gloves, is legendary. Also that Talleyrand was only thanks to Carême – as well as Talleyrand's beautiful niece – able to get the best settlement for defeated France at the Congress of Vienna in 1814/15: While Talleyrand wooed the Congress, Carême cooked his heart out and orchestrated huge kitchen brigades to gastronomically seduce and appease the European heads of state. What turn might world history have taken, one wonders, if the soup had been too salty and the partridges burnt? Not a legend, but a fact, is that the power of food – the power of the grand dining table and the impressive banquet – has always been a politically effective instrument. What else were the culinary orgies of the Roman Empire but scheming power games? How else but with overindulgent lust could the powerful of this world be charmed? Where else but at a common dining table, breaking bread and sharing wine, could matters – between the lines, of course – be referred to or even discussed, or yes, even settled, which could not even be approached otherwise?

Just how closely the art of cooking is linked with the art of politics is confirmed by the many statesmanlike names that can be found on menus: for example, chateaubriand, a double tenderloin steak, which was named after the French author and foreign minister François René Vicomte de Chateaubriand. The egg dish "Œufs au plat Metternich" was dedicated to Prince Metternich, the head of the Congress of Vienna. Paul Bocuse, who is not (yet) one of the classic chefs, created a legendary soup topped with a puff pastry crust and christened it "Soupe Giscard d'Estaing" to celebrate the election of Valéry Giscard d'Estaing as president of France in the year 1974. But not only great statesmen have been honoured with gastronomic tributes – Escoffier, the brilliant cooking reformer, dedicated his most famous dishes especially to the women he adored: For the legendary actress Sarah Bernhardt he originated "Les fraises Sarah Bernhardt," for Madame Melba, the Australian opera diva, he created "Pêches Melba," and he indulged singer Adelina Parti with a special chicken dish which later carried her name.

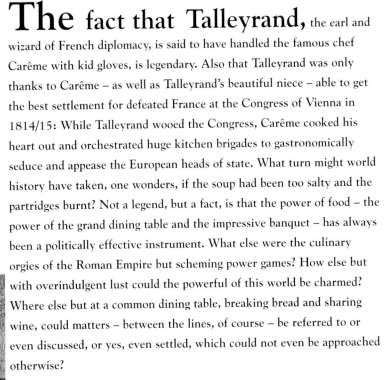

Sarah Bernhardt, the great French tragic actress, was also an appreciative fan of Escoffier's cookery – and Escoffier appreciated the diva, although she was generally feared for her moodiness and fits of temper. In whatever hotels she stayed, she attracted attention. Only a single waiter, to whom she gave exact instructions beforehand, was allowed to serve her. One story tells of how the waiter Sarah Bernhardt had selected, of all people, was fired on the spot by César Ritz because of some trivial matter. When the actress found out about this at dinner time, she screamed and fussed so vehemently that Ritz had the lowly waiter found and brought back to the restaurant so that she could dine as she was accustomed. Escoffier dedicated his strawberry creation "Les fraises Sarah Bernhardt" to her.

Auguste Escoffier at the Hotel Ritz, Paris

Brillat-Savarin (1755–1826)

Jean-Anthelme Brillat-Savarin, son of an old, well-to-do family of lawyers, studied jurisprudence, chemistry, physics and medicine. He dreamed of a life of pleasure and contemplation, but it turned out otherwise. As a civil magistrate, his life was endangered with the outbreak of the French Revolution, and he had to flee France. Brillat-Savarin travelled around Germany, Switzerland and the United States and was able to support himself – since he was fluent in five languages – as a language and music teacher. On the side, he studied philosophy and gastronomy. "When I came to consider the pleasures of the table in all their aspects, I soon perceived that something better than a mere cookery book might be made of such a subject," said Savarin in justifying his treatise *The Physiology of Taste*, which he published anonymously in 1825. The book caused a stir and heralded the age of the culinary chronicler. His theory, "Man has to eat, just like every other living thing, but it is the will of Nature that man should eat well," has become an accepted fact. Brillat-Savarin's theory was that it is the sense of taste which brings people the maximum of delight:

Because the pleasure of eating is the only one which, enjoyed in moderation, is not followed by weariness.

Because it is of all times, all ages, and all conditions.

Because it recurs of necessity at least once a day, and may without inconvenience be repeated twice or three times within the same space of time.

Because it can be enjoyed in company with all our other pleasures, and can even console us for their absence.

Because the impressions which it receives are at once more durable and more dependent on our will.

And lastly, because when we eat, we experience an undefinable and peculiar sensation of well being

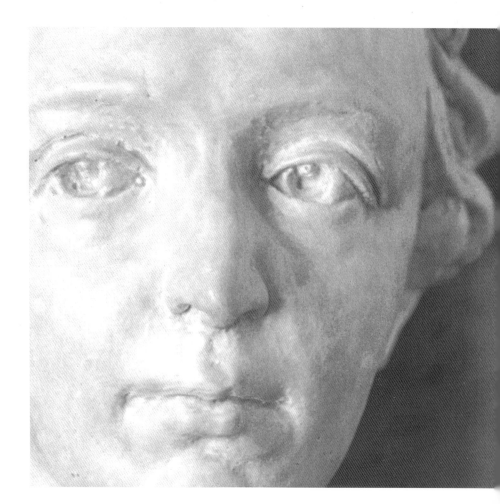

Antoine
Marie Carême (1783–1835)

Carême was the youngest in a family of twenty-five siblings – no wonder, then, that his father informed him at age twelve that he would have to seek his own fortune. Since the young Carême knew nothing but hunger, he found himself a job as an apprentice in a public kitchen. He was ambitious and was not satisfied until he was able to perfect his craft to the point where he was one of the best chefs of his era. At that time the presentation of food was undergoing a major change – all of the dishes now had to be on the table when the guests came into the dining hall. What we today call a buffet had been born. In the meantime, Carême had learned to draw at a Parisian copperplate engraving studio and developed increasingly artistic compositions for the different food items, which all had a re-lationship to each other and were arranged according to colour. The admiration for this new style of table setting was great, although many of the foods were cold by the time they could be eaten, and – since the compositions were not moveable – the guests, who were seated, could only enjoy what was within their reach. Later on, Carême worked for Talleyrand for twelve years and also accompanied him to the Congress of Vienna, where he excelled with culinary flights of fancy à la Carême. After that, his path led to London, Paris, Moscow and back to Paris: As a culinary artist, it was only there that he found paradise. Carême, the cel-ebrated artist, was a fanatic, and his perception of the world was a world which was reduced to culinary terms – Russia meant caviar, Germany was strawberries, the change of seasons signaled only the change from game to new potatoes. After thirty years of uninterrupted work, his health was failing, and until his death in the year 1835, Carême devoted himself to his literary works. His fame outlived him, since he is considered the true founder of *Grande Cuisine*.

Auguste Escoffier

(1846–1935)

Before Auguste Escoffier became the great Escoffier of gastronomic history, he had to learn the hard way – but these experiences later helped him to revolutionise cooking and the job profile of professional chefs. Kitchen work was especially hard for Auguste, since he was quite short. He had to wear special shoes to even be able to work at the stove. He suffered from the teasing he was subjected to and from the unbearable heat of the oven. At that time, kitchen conditions were catastrophic – cooks were considered domestic help and slaved away for fourteen hours a day or more. The kitchens were badly constructed, with no way for either steam or smoke to escape. Most cooks drank huge quantities of beer to quench their thirst, which was quite detrimental to the quality of the meals and the working climate. Auguste Escoffier resolved that if he ever became head chef, he would see to it that those conditions would change, and cruelty and drunkenness would be banned from his kitchen. It was a resolution that he was soon able to put into

action. Meeting legendary hotelier Cäsar Ritz was fateful for Escoffier – the two complemented each other in their passion to offer their guests only the best. Ritz and Escoffier were a brilliant team. They celebrated their greatest triumphs in London, where they became "the culinary pied pipers of society." The crème de la crème – English princes, Russian grand dukes and the great stars of the theatre and opera – dined with them. Escoffier also understood and complied with his business and theatre customers' wish for faster service. He radically changed the whole kitchen system and simplified the service. The kitchen brigade was divided into separate work stations, unlike before, when a team had cooked the whole menu. With this change, he laid the foundation for a system that restaurants still use today. At the same time, among other things, Escoffier made sure there was good ventilation, eschewed gas and aluminum in favour of cooking only on wood or charcoal fires with copper pans, forbid profanity, tobacco and alcohol consumption during working hours, and made sure that his employees were also neat and orderly off the job – because he recognised already back then that well-groomed personnel contribute to the image of the establishment they represent.

Notre Dame de Paris

Gastronomic Stories that Made History

Between 1814 and 1816 Carême arranged gigantic banquets for the Bourbons – once he converted the great hall of the Louvre into a kitchen to serve 1200 guests. At a dinner on the Champs Elysées for ten thousand people (!), he prepared a menu using 75 calves, 6 cows, 250 sheep, 8000 turkeys, 2000 fattened turkey hens, 1000 chickens, 1000 partridges, 500 hams, 500 tongues, 1000 pies, 1000 "babas" (raisin cakes) and 1000 carp. The guests drank 18,000 bottles and 145 carafes of wine with the food.

It is not an exaggeration to say that gourmets and bon vivants prevented state bankruptcy after the collapse of Napoleonic France. Brillat-Savarin wrote that the victorious powers "brought with them huge appetites and stomachs of remarkable calibre and were not satisfied with the official food and service, but rather were drawn to nobler fare. Soon Paris was one big restaurant …"

After France declared war on Germany in 1870, Napoleon III landed in a Prussian prison. Paris was occupied. The director of the zoo on the Bois de Boulogne decided to kill his precious animals so that they would not have to starve to death – to the delight of the city's chefs, who could now create new, expensive menus with exotic ingredients. For Christmas dinner at "Voisin" guests were served, among other things, stuffed donkey's head, elephant broth, roast camel English style, peppered kangaroo ragout, bear chops, leg of wolf and antelope paté with truffles.

Source: Seifert-Samtschek, *Die Kochkunst in zwei Jahrtausenden*

Fillet of Beef "Helder"

Recipe by Wolfgang Kuchler

500g potatoes
butter for frying

100ml Madeira
100ml well reduced, dark veal stock
(see recipe page 192)
salt and freshly ground pepper

Béarnaise sauce:
150g butter
3 tbsp white wine mixed with a little
tarragon vinegar
50g shallots, finely chopped
10 peppercorns, crushed
2 egg yolks
salt, lemon juice,
cayenne pepper
1 tbs finely chopped tarragon
and chervil

500g fillet of beef cut from
the centre of the fillet
2 tbsp clarified butter
or a mixture of butter
and oil
salt and freshly
ground pepper

Garnish:
1 large tomato, peeled,
seeded and diced
a pinch of sugar
1 tbsp extra-virgin olive oil

This elaborate meat dish was named for the Dutch city Den Helder in memory of the ship battle between the Anglo-French fleet and the Dutch in the year 1673.

To **clarify** (e.g. stock) means to remove all impurities from a liquid. To clarify butter, bring it as slowly as possible over gentle heat to a steady simmer. The whey (white solids) will sink to the bottom, and scum will rise to the top. Take care not to stir it. Skim off the scum, carefully spoon out or pour off the clarified butter, leaving behind the milky white solids.

1 Peel the potatoes and cut out nicely rounded shapes using a melon baller. Rinse and blanch in boiling salted water. Toss in hot butter until cooked, season and keep them warm.

2 For the Madeira sauce, put the Madeira in a small pan and reduce to almost nothing. Add the veal stock and simmer to a coating consistency. Whisk in a knob of butter if wished. Keep warm.

3 For the Béarnaise sauce, clarify the butter and keep it warm. Bring the wine and vinegar to a boil in a small pan with the shallots and peppercorns. Allow to cool. Whisk in the egg yolks, place the pan over simmering water and continue to beat until thick and creamy and the mixture drops heavily from the whisk. Remove the pan from the simmering water and beat in the clarified, warm butter over gentle heat. Season carefully and add lemon juice and cayenne pepper to taste. Stir in the herbs. The sauce can be kept warm for only a limited time.

4 Cut the fillet in 4 equal-sized pieces. Fry on both sides in the clarified butter or butter and oil until just done but still nicely pink inside. Keep warm.

5 For the garnish, fry the tomato cubes gently in a little olive oil with a pinch of sugar.

6 Put a tablespoon of Béarnaise sauce in the middle of each plate, place the sliced fillet on top and spoon some Madeira sauce over. Garnish with the tomato cubes and Parisienne potatoes.

Sole Strips Prince Murat

Recipe by Wolfgang Kuchler

500g skinless, boneless sole fillets
salt and freshly ground pepper
lemon juice
2 tbsp chopped parsley
2 potatoes, peeled and cut in cubes
2 cooked artichoke hearts, trimmed and cut in cubes
plain white flour
50g butter
1 large tomato, peeled, seeded and cubed
4 tbsp thick gravy from a meat roast, hot

1 Cut the sole fillets in finger-sized strips, season with salt, pepper and lemon juice and mix with half the chopped parsley.

2 Blanch the potato cubes and fry them briefly in a little of the butter. Do the same with the artichoke hearts.

3 Toss the sole strips in a little flour. Heat some more butter and brown them on both sides. Add the fried potato and artichoke cubes and the tomato dice and cook them all together briefly.

4 Heat the remaining butter until foaming, mix in the rest of the parsley. Arrange the fish, potatoes and artichokes on well warmed plates, pour the parsley butter over and drizzle some gravy around.

Autumn Soup Carême

Recipe by Roland Jöhri

125g leeks, white part only
2 sticks celery
a quarter of a lettuce

1 litre + 100ml consommé
2 tbsp plain white flour
75g peas
a pinch of sugar
salt and freshly ground pepper
2 egg yolks
4 tbsp whipping cream

Croutons:
3 slices white bread, crusts removed, cut in cubes
50g butter

1 Slice the leeks, celery and lettuce finely, wash and drain.

2 Mix 100ml of the consommé to a paste with the flour and stir until quite smooth. Bring the rest of the consommé to the boil and gradually stir in the consommé and flour mixture. Simmer for 2–3 minutes. Add the leek, celery, lettuce and peas, season with sugar and pepper and simmer for 15–20 minutes more, or until the vegetables are just tender. Season the soup and stir in the yolks and cream to thicken. Do not allow the soup to boil again.

3 For the croutons, fry the bread cubes in the butter until golden brown.

4 Pour the soup into soup bowls and serve the croutons separately.

Poule-au-Pot Henri IV

Recipe by Roland Jöhri

1½ litres chicken stock
a 2kg boiling fowl, or 1 Bresse chicken

100g leeks, sliced
50g celeriac, cut in batons
100g carrots, cut in batons
100g cabbage, cut in thick strips
1 bay leaf
2 cloves
salt and freshly ground pepper
flat-leaved parsley

1 Bring the stock to a boil in a saucepan. Put the boiling fowl or Bresse chicken in another pan and cover with water. Bring to a boil, tip away the water and replace it with the boiling stock. Add the vegetables, bay leaf and cloves and season to taste. Simmer very gently for about 1½ hours until the meat starts to come away from the bones. Test occasionally for tenderness with a skewer. Lift out the fowl, carve it in pieces and put them back in the pan. Check the seasoning and garnish with parsley just before serving.

Veal Chops Talleyrand

Recipe by Roland Jöhri

4 veal chops on the bone,
each about 150g
2 tbsp peanut oil
salt and freshly
ground pepper

Chicken stuffing:
200g boneless chicken breast,
trimmed
2 shallots, chopped
5 tbsp *crème fraîche*
a walnut-sized truffle (about 25g),
cut in tiny dice

a 150g piece of caul, soaked in cold
water and squeezed out
50g melted butter

1 Season the chops and brown on both sides in the hot oil. Leave to cool.

2 Cut the chicken breast in small pieces and chill it thoroughly. Process it briefly in a food processor with the shallots until smooth. Gradually work in the *crème fraîche*. Season with salt and pepper. Stir in the diced truffle with a wooden spoon.

3 Spread the chops on both sides with a little of the chicken mixture, wrap in caul. Melt the butter and fry the chops gently in it on both sides till lightly golden. Both chops and the filling should be just cooked and hot through.

4 Serve on plates with pasta (macaroni).

Tip:
A truffle
jus goes
well with
this dish.

Peach Melba

Recipe by Roland Jöhri

4 ripe white-fleshed peaches
100g caster sugar

200g raspberries
400g vanilla ice cream (see recipe for
Coupe Nesselrode page 81)
4 tbsp flaked almonds

1 Plunge the peaches in boiling water for a
few seconds, remove and place them in iced water.
Peel, halve and stone them, and put them on a plate
sprinkled with half the sugar. Chill.

2 Purée the raspberries. Add the rest of
the sugar and push through a sieve.

3 Arrange eight scoops of ice cream on a
chilled serving dish. Put the halved peaches on top,
pour over the raspberry purée and sprinkle with
flaked almonds.

Tip:
If wished,
the dessert
can be de-
corated with
whipped
cream, mint
leaves and
extra rasp-
berries.

Nellie Melba (1861–1931) was a cel-
ebrated Australian soprano. She
was one of Escoffier's favourite
guests. During one of her frequent
diets, Escoffier created Melba toast
and Peach Melba for her.

500g ripe strawberries
3 tbsp Curaçao
200ml whipping cream
a little icing sugar
4 scoops vanilla ice cream
shredded mint leaves to garnish

Strawberry Rosett Romanoff

Recipe by Wolfgang Kuchler

1 Wash, hull and slice the strawberries and put them in a bowl with the Curaçao to marinate.

2 Whip the cream softly with the icing sugar and divide it between the plates. Fan out the strawberry slices like rose petals on top and finish with a scoop of ice cream. Sprinkle if wished with more icing sugar and garnish with mint leaves.

Coupe Nesselrode
Recipe by Roland Jöhri

Vanilla Ice Cream:
3 vanilla pods
8 egg yolks
200g caster sugar
800ml milk
200ml double cream

Chestnut 'vermicelli':
250g chestnut purée
200ml Kirsch
150ml whipping cream

4 meringues

1 For the ice cream, split the vanilla pods and scrape out the seeds and soft insides. Mix these with the yolks and sugar in a bowl and beat until thoroughly light and mousse-like. Bring the milk and the cream to the boil and add it to the egg mixture, stirring. Put it back in the pan and bring to just below boiling, stirring constantly, until it thickens enough to coat the back of a wooden spoon. Strain the custard and put it in the freezer for about 10 minutes. Remove and stir it thoroughly, then return it to the freezer. Repeat this process four or five times, to prevent uneven freezing and formation of ice crystals.

2 For the 'vermicelli', mix the Kirsch into the chestnut purée. Beat the cream till stiff and fold in all but 5 tablespoons. Put the mixture in a 'vermicelli' extruder.

3 Place a meringue on each plate. Arrange one scoop of vanilla ice cream on each one and squeeze squiggles of chestnut purée ('vermicelli') all over the top. Decorate with the reserved whipped cream.

Crêpes Suzette
Recipe by Wolfgang Kuchler

50g plain white flour, sifted
1 level tbsp caster sugar
a pinch of salt
2 tbsp whipping cream
5 tbsp milk
1 egg
15g butter, melted
thin strips of lemon and orange zest
1 tbsp Cognac
1 tbsp finely chopped macaroons
butter for frying the crêpes

75g caster sugar
75g butter
6 sugar lumps, rubbed over an orange
400ml freshly squeezed orange juice
100ml Cognac and Grand Marnier

1 Mix together thoroughly the flour, sugar and salt. Add the milk and cream and mix to a smooth batter. Stir in the egg, melted butter, lemon and orange zest, Cognac and macaroon crumbs. Heat a crêpe pan and brush with a little butter. Make thin crêpes (allow 2–3 per person). Keep them warm.

2 Dissolve the sugar in a small, heavy pan and cook it to a light caramel. Add the butter, and before it goes brown add the flavoured sugar lumps and the orange juice, Cognac and Grand Marnier. Dip the crêpes in this mixture and set them alight. Arrange on serving plates and pour the sauce over.

Rice:
200ml milk
1 vanilla pod
50g pudding rice (e.g. Vialone)
a pinch of salt
50g caster sugar

Cream:
4 leaves gelatine,
soaked in cold water
2 egg yolks
1 tbsp milk
50g caster sugar
400ml whipping cream

Fruit Sauce:
100g raspberries
50g caster sugar

Cold Rice Cream

Recipe from Confiserie Sprüngli

1 Heat the milk with the vanilla pod. Remove the vanilla pod, split it open, scrape out the seeds and put them back in the milk. Add the rice, salt and sugar and cook gently, stirring constantly, until the rice is tender (about 15 minutes). Cover with clingfilm and allow to cool.

2 Mix together the egg yolks, milk and sugar and heat them gently in a small pan without allowing them to boil. Remove immediately from the heat and drop in the squeezed out gelatine leaves. Stir to mix well. Allow the mixture to cool, then stir it into the rice. Whip the cream till stiff and fold it in. Line a mould with foil or baking paper and pour in the rice cream. Chill for 5–6 hours.

3 For the fruit sauce, boil the raspberries briefly with the sugar until the juice runs and blend in the liquidiser till smooth. Push through a sieve to eliminate pips.

4 Run the mould under hot water and turn out the rice cream. Cut nice slices with a big knife, arrange them on plates and surround with the sauce.

Champagne Profiteroles

Recipe from Confiserie Sprüngli

Gives about 35–40 profiteroles

Choux Pastry:
350ml water
75g butter
a pinch of salt
3 tbsp caster sugar
175g plain white flour
4–5 eggs

Cream:
2 egg yolks
1 tbsp milk
250g caster sugar
2 leaves gelatine, soaked in cold water
2 tbsp Champagne
400ml whipping cream

1 For the choux pastry, bring together to a boil the water, butter, salt and sugar. Reduce the heat. Add the flour all in one go and stir vigorously with a wooden spoon until a dough forms and it starts to come away from the bottom of the pan. Cool a little, then stir in the eggs one by one. After the fourth egg, check the consistency: it should be soft, but not at all runny. If necessary, add the last egg.

2 Heat the oven to 180ºC/Gas 4. Put the pastry into a forcing bag fitted with a large, smooth nozzle. Pipe walnut-sized blobs, well spaced out, onto a baking sheet lined with non-stick baking paper. Bake them for 15 minutes, then reduce the oven temperature to 150ºC/Gas 2 and continue baking for 40 minutes. Important: do not open the oven door while the profiteroles are baking. Remove and cool on a rack.

3 For the champagne cream, put the egg yolks, milk and 50g of the sugar in a small pan and heat very gently. The mixture must not boil. Remove immediately from the stove. Squeeze out the gelatine leaves and drop them into the pan. Stir to dissolve. Mix in the champagne and allow to cool somewhat. Whip the cream till stiff, fold it into the champagne cream. Put into a forcing bag.

4 Make a hole in the bottom of the profiteroles, fill with the champagne cream and chill for about 1 hour.

5 Make a caramel with some of the remaining sugar in a saucepan, stirring constantly. Add more sugar and allow to melt. Arrange the profiteroles on a serving dish, using the caramel to stick them together. Garnish as wished. Chill for 3 hours.

Sprüngli

– The Sweet Classic on Zurich's Bahnhofstrasse

The internationally famous Confiserie Sprüngli, which is as much of a Zurich landmark as the Grossmünster Church or Sechseläuten, proves that classics can definitely be modern.

The sweet history began over 160 years ago, when David Sprüngli purchased a confectionery shop in the middle of what is now Zurich's Old Town. When those quarters became too cramped, he moved his operation to the other side of the river onto Paradeplatz. Besides the shop and the bakery, he set up a refreshment room – which at the time, in the year 1859, was an absolute novelty in Zurich. Women were welcome there even when they weren't accompanied by a man.

Charlotte Royale
Recipe from Confiserie Sprüngli

Sponge Cake
(for a baking tray 40 x 35cm):
5 eggs, separated
100g sugar
25g plain white flour
25g cornflour

Cream:
2 egg yolks
1 tbsp milk
50g caster sugar
4 leaves gelatine, soaked in cold water
400g strawberries
400ml whipping cream

raspberry jam
apricot jam, sieved

1 For the sponge cake, line the baking tray with non-stick paper and heat the oven to 230ºC/Gas 8. Beat together in the electric mixer the yolks and 50g sugar until thoroughly well creamed. Beat 4 of the whites with half the rest of the sugar until stiff. Sprinkle on the rest of the sugar and continue beating until glossy. Sift together the flour and cornflour. Fold the egg yolk mixture carefully into the whites and then fold in the flour and cornflour. Tip the mixture into the prepared baking tray and smooth the top with a palette knife. Bake in the middle of the oven for 5–8 minutes or until just firm and pale golden.

2 Invert the cake onto a second sheet of baking paper, lay a damp cloth over the baking paper on the underside of the cake and peel off the paper. Cover with the inverted baking tray and let it cool. (This way it does not dry out and remains pliable.)

3 Cut out a base from the edge of the cooled sponge sheet to fit the chosen mould or bowl. Spread the rest of the sponge sheet thinly with raspberry jam, cut in half lengthwise and roll up firmly to form two rolls. Put the rolls in the freezer briefly to firm them up, then cut them in ½cm slices. Line the mould with foil, place the base in the bottom and arrange the slices tightly together around the edge so that the filling cannot leak out.

4 For the cream, put the egg yolks, milk and sugar in a pan and beat vigorously over gentle heat without allowing them to boil. Squeeze out the gelatine and stir them into the warm cream. Remove the cream from the heat and beat over cold water.

5 Blend half the strawberries to a rough purée in a liquidiser or food processor and chop the rest roughly. Whip the cream till stiff, and fold it into the cream with the strawberries. Pour into the prepared mould and chill for 3–4 hours or until set.

6 Dip the mould briefly in hot water and turn out the charlotte onto a plate. Heat the apricot jam and glaze the charlotte with it. Garnish as wished.

The Sprüngli family was very innovative. Thus, in time, the Sprüngli dynasty became one of the leading pioneers in the processing of chocolate. But over the decades, Confiserie Sprüngli has also led the way in the field of recipe and product development and is now a leading speciality shop.

Today this success story is being written by the sixth generation of Sprünglis – always with the awareness that the time-honoured fundamentals still apply: maintaining the tradition of skilled craftsmanship and meeting the highest standards of quality. With its 550 employees, Sprüngli is one of the largest and most modern confectionery producers in Europe.

Sprüngli has developed a new "truffes" line made with organic cocoa especially for natural**gourmet**, which is available both at Confiserie Sprüngli on Paradeplatz and from Natural Gourmet Cooking.

Confiserie Sprüngli, Paradeplatz, 8022 Zurich
Telephone +41 1 221 17 22, Fax +41 1 211 34 35

Navigating through the Cuisine of the Far East

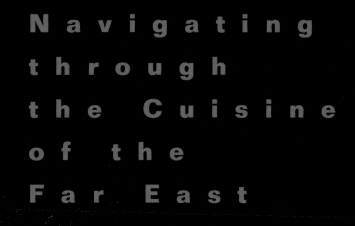

The shade of

the pine

depends on

the clarity of

the moon.

The good cook

Prince Wen Hui's cook was carving up an ox. Every touch of his hand, every heave of his shoulder, every step of his foot, every thrust of his knee, with the slicing and parting of the flesh, and the zinging of the knife – all was in perfect rhythm, just like the Dance of the Mulberry Grove or a part in the Ching Shou symphony.

Prince Wen Hui remarked, "How wonderfully you have mastered your art." The cook laid down his knife and said, "What your servant really cares for is Tao, which goes beyond mere art. When I first began to cut up oxen, I saw nothing but oxen. After three years of practicing, I no longer saw the ox as a whole. I now work with my spirit, not with my eyes. My senses stop functioning and my spirit takes over. I follow the natural grain, letting the knife find its way through the many hidden openings, taking advantage of what is there, never touching a ligament or tendon, much less a main joint.

"A good cook changes his knife once a year because he cuts, while a mediocre cook has to change his every month because he hacks. I've had this knife of mine for nineteen years and have cut up thousands of oxen with it, and yet the edge is as if it were fresh from the grindstone. There are spaces between the joints. The blade of the knife has no thickness. That which has no thickness has plenty of room to pass through these spaces. Therefore, after nineteen years, my blade is as sharp as ever. However, when I come to a difficulty, I size up the joint, look carefully, keep my eyes on what I am doing, and work slowly. Then with a very slight movement of the knife, I cut the whole ox wide open. It falls apart like a clod of earth crumbling to the ground. I stand there with the knife in my hand, looking about me with a feeling of accomplishment and delight. Then I wipe the knife clean and put it away."

"Well done!" said the Prince. "From the words of my cook, I have learned the secret of growth." *Tschuang Tsu – Inner Chapters*

"We are right on course," says the captain. "Our current position is 18° north, 99° east, and we will be flying over Cheng Mai, Thailand, in a few minutes. As scheduled, our arrival in Hong Kong will be in two hours and forty-five minutes." I, a passenger on Flight SR 170 Zurich–Bombay–Hong Kong, sit as scheduled in Seat 6C and am also on course. It feels good. I know my coordinates. 18° north, 99° east. I know where I am. I am up in the sky and am navigating through a night that will last longer than all others before it. 18° north, 99° east. I am on course to Cassiopeia, the wondrous one from my childhood dreams. Castor and Pollux beckon to me from afar, while Orion, the mythical hunter, reels blindly through the Milky Way toward the sun wielding a heavy sword. Where, for Heaven's sake, are Phosphoros and Hesperus, the ancient Greeks? In what spiral arms of the galaxy are they hiding? There, behind Cassiopeia, the globular clusters of Andromeda can already be seen. Joyfully, I cast star talers through space. Flat and buzzing, they skip over the invisible surface until they are sucked in by black holes or are split into a billion sparks by exploding quasars; red giant stars expand and contract, eventually becoming white dwarf stars – a round dance of shooting stars; a giant cosmic fireworks display fills every corner of the galaxy and rains down on me – "... landing as scheduled in a few minutes. Enjoy your stay, and don't forget to explore the culinary cosmos of Far Eastern cooking while you are here." I, as scheduled in Seat 6C, observe with a degree of distraction a shiny square lying in my lap and decide that it is a good omen for a further excursion into another (g)astronomic galaxy.

Postscript: The culinary cosmos of the East was really like a dream. The one and only thing that brought me back to earth and reality was that shiny farewell – the galactic greeting was sweet and tasted like Swiss chocolate.

庖丁為文惠君解牛手之所觸肩之所倚足之所履膝之所踦砉然嚮然奏刀騞然莫不中音合於桑林之舞乃中經首之會文惠君曰譆善哉技蓋至此乎庖丁釋刀對曰臣之所好者道也進乎技矣始臣之解牛之時所見無非牛者三年之後未嘗見全牛也方今之時臣以神遇而不以目視官知止而神欲行依乎天理批大郤導大窾因其固然技經肯綮之未嘗而況大軱乎良庖歲更刀割也族庖月更刀折也今臣之刀十九年矣所解數千牛矣而刀刃若新發於硎彼節者有間而刀刃者無厚以無厚入有間恢恢乎其於遊刃必有餘地矣是以十九年而刀刃若新發於硎雖然每至於族吾見其難為怵然為戒視為止行為遲動刀甚微謋然已解如土委地提刀而立為之四顧為之躊躇滿志善刀而藏之文惠君曰善哉吾聞庖丁之言得養生焉

Sushi

Recipe by Rolf von Siebenthal

75g Japanese Hikari rice
100ml water
1 tbsp rice vinegar, mixed with a little sugar and salt

4 slices fresh raw salmon fillet
4 medium giant prawns, split in half lengthwise, black intestines removed
a little wasabi paste (green horseradish mustard)

1 Wash the rice in several changes of water, then soak in water for 1 hour. Drain, put in a pan with 100ml water and bring to a boil. Reduce the heat and cook gently until all the water is evaporated. Remove from the heat and leave to stand, covered, for 10 minutes. Then remove the lid and allow it to cool to lukewarm. Mix the rice vinegar into the warm rice, chill.

2 Press the rice into 8 little oval-shaped pieces. Brush the prawns and salmon with a little wasabi paste and lay on top of the prepared sushi.

3 Serve the sushi with a little curl of wasabi paste.

Vietnamese Spring Rolls with Orange Dipping Sauce

Recipe by Rolf von Siebenthal

Makes 8 spring rolls – serve one each for a first course, and freeze the rest

25g soya vermicelli (cellophane noodles)
25g shiitake mushrooms, sliced
1 spring onion, finely sliced
½ a carrot, cut in thin strips
50g bean sprouts
1 shallot, finely sliced
2 cloves garlic, chopped
a little finely chopped fresh chili
a sprig of fresh coriander
3 tbsp oil
100g chicken breast, cut in thin strips
100g cocktail shrimps
2 tbsp sherry
2 tbsp soy sauce
2 tbsp oyster sauce
1 egg
a pinch of sugar
salt and freshly ground pepper

8 rice pancakes about 2 x 2cm
8 unblemished lettuce leaves, ribs removed
½ an egg to glaze
oil for frying

Orange Dipping Sauce:
1 orange
2 tbsp soy sauce
3 tbsp hoisin sauce
1 tbsp sesame oil
100ml light veal stock (see recipe page 192)
cayenne pepper

1 Soak the soya vermicelli briefly, drain and cut them in two or three pieces. Soften all the vegetables in the oil with the chillies and coriander, add the chicken and shrimps and cook together gently. Stir in the vermicelli and cook together briefly. Moisten with the sherry, soy sauce and oyster sauce and allow to evaporate completely. Beat the egg and mix it in, add the sugar and season to taste.

2 Lay the rice pancakes between damp teatowels or spray with water so that they become pliable. Put a lettuce leaf on each pancake, and fill with the prepared vegetables. Turn the ends in and roll the pancakes up tightly. Brush with egg so that they do not unroll. Deep fry in hot oil.

3 For the orange dipping sauce, cut strips of zest from the orange with a zester or sharp knife; squeeze out the juice – you should have 3 tablespoons.

4 Blanch the zest strips. Boil the orange juice with the soy sauce, hoisin sauce, sesame oil and stock and reduce to about 150ml. Season with a little cayenne pepper and stir in the blanched zest.

Mulligatawny Soup

Recipe by Wolfgang Kuchler

25g butter
2 tbsp olive oil
100g shallots, thinly sliced
½ clove garlic, mashed
½ an apple, thinly sliced
25g curry powder
1 litre chicken stock
100ml unsweetened coconut milk
a bouquet garni (parsley and celery leaves)
100ml whipping cream

Garnishes:
rice, chicken pieces, toasted coconut flakes

1 Melt the butter with the oil and soften the shallots, garlic and apple gently without allowing them to brown. Sprinkle on the curry powder and pour in the stock and coconut milk. Add the bouquet garni and let the soup simmer for 30 minutes.

2 Remove the bouquet garni. Add the cream to the soup, blend till smooth in the liquidiser, strain and season to taste. Stir in the garnishes and serve at once.

Chicken Curry with Basmati Rice

Recipe by Rolf von Siebenthal

2 free-range spring chickens, each about
450g
salt and freshly ground pepper

3 large cloves garlic, sliced
2 tbsp oil
200g onions, sliced
1 rounded tsp red curry powder
½ tsp chat masala
½ tsp ground cumin
1 tbsp tomato purée
300ml light veal stock
(see recipe page 192)
3 tbsp natural yogurt
a sprig of fresh coriander

Basmati Rice:
½ litre water
1 Indian bay leaf
(or 1 ordinary bay leaf)
250g Basmati rice

1 Heat the oven to 200ºC/Gas 6.
Season the spring chickens inside and out,
truss and roast them for 20–25 minutes or
until golden brown. Cut each one in 4 pieces
(2 legs, 2 pieces of breast) and remove all bones
(except for the wing bones).

2 Fry the garlic in the oil till lightly col-
oured, add the onions and cook till golden brown.
Add all the spices and cook together briefly. Moisten with the stock, add the tomato purée, bring to
a boil and simmer for about 10 minutes. Blend till
smooth in the liquidiser or food processor. Put
back in the pan, add the yogurt and bring back
very briefly to a boil. Stir the coriander into the
sauce and season to taste.

3 For the rice, bring the water to a boil
with salt and the bay leaf. Add the rice, bring
back to the boil, reduce the heat to a bare mini-
mum, cover and leave to steep for 15 minutes.

Tip:
**Fried
bananas,
chutney
and sliced
cucumbers
can be
served with
this dish.**

92

Lemongrass Quiche with Giant Prawns

Recipe by Rolf von Siebenthal

For a 22cm-diameter quiche tin, 2cm deep

150g plain white flour
50g soft butter
2 tbsp water
2 tbsp double cream
salt
butter for the tin

1 lemongrass stem
a small piece of fresh ginger
1 spring onion
15g butter
a large bunch of chives, chopped
2 small eggs
200ml double cream

150g giant prawns
15g grated Parmesan
salt and freshly ground pepper

1 Put the flour in a bowl and make a well in the centre. Add the soft butter, water, cream and salt and work up to a dough. Let the dough rest for a little before using. Roll it out, lay it in the buttered quiche tin and leave to rest again for about half an hour.

2 Slice the lemongrass, ginger and spring onion very finely and soften briefly in the butter. Add the chives. Mix the eggs and cream together and add to the lemongrass mixture. Mix together well and season to taste.

3 Heat the oven to 200°C/Gas 6. Split the prawns in half lengthwise and cut each one in two pieces. Season lightly and put them in the pastry case. Stir the custard and pour it over the prawns. Sprinkle with Parmesan and bake the quiche for 25–30 minutes or until just set and pale golden.

Chilled Apple and Horseradish Soup with Marinated Salmon

Recipe by Roland Jöhri

2 apples
2 shallots
½ a fennel bulb
olive oil
1.5 litres fish stock (see recipe page 192)
2 tbsp fresh, grated horseradish
100ml whipping cream
100ml sour cream
a little lemon juice
200g marinated salmon

Tip: Smoked fish can be used instead of marinated salmon.

1 Slice the apples, shallots and fennel very finely and sweat them all together in a little olive oil. Add the fish stock. (Substitute white wine, water and salt for the fish stock, if you prefer – bring to a boil and use as above.)

2 Add the horseradish and cook until the vegetables are tender. Boil down to reduce the liquid to about 400ml. Add the cream, sour cream and lemon juice and blend until smooth. Strain and chill the soup. Cut the marinated salmon in small cubes, divide between chilled soup bowls and pour the soup over. Serve well chilled.

Fried Rice with Duck

Recipe by Rolf von Siebenthal

200g skinless, boneless duck breast, trimmed and cut in strips
2 tbsp unsalted soy sauce
a small piece fresh ginger, chopped
2 cloves garlic, mashed
1 tsp cornflour

250g Basmati rice
½ litre water
100g mangetout (sugar snap peas), fresh or frozen
1–2 carrots, peeled
2 handfuls fresh spinach
2 spring onions
a little fresh red chili, to taste

2 tbsp peanut oil
2 eggs
2 tbsp sesame oil
75g water chestnuts, sliced
salt and freshly ground pepper

1 Mix together the soy sauce, ginger, garlic and cornflour and marinate the duck in it in the refrigerator for 1 hour.

2 Bring the water to a boil with a little salt, add the rice, bring back to the boil, reduce the heat, cover and leave to steep for 15 minutes. Drain.

3 Halve the mangetout, cut the carrots and spinach in strips, slice the spring onions and chop the chili finely.

4 Sear the duck strips in a little hot oil and remove from the heat. Beat the eggs with the sesame oil, add to the pan and fry, stirring, until the eggs set and form pale golden strands. Add the rice and vegetables, stirring constantly. Add the duck to the pan again, cook together briefly till hot through. Taste for seasoning.

a 500g piece of fillet of beef

50g fresh chillies, seeds removed
2 shallots
2 cloves garlic
a walnut-sized piece of ginger, peeled
2 tsp turmeric
5 tbsp unsweetened coconut milk
a little lemongrass
a bay leaf

250g courgettes, halved and seeded
butter
2 tbsp oil

1 Chop the chillies, garlic, ginger, shallots and turmeric together to a rough paste. Spread this mixture onto the beef, cover and marinate in the refrigerator for 24 hours.

2 Scrape the marinade off the beef and put it in a small pan with the coconut milk, lemongrass and bay leaf. Bring to a boil and simmer for 20 minutes. Discard the lemongrass and bay leaf, blend the sauce till smooth in the liquidiser and check the seasoning.

3 Cut the unpeeled courgette in even-sized strips and toss them in a little hot butter. Moisten with a little of the sauce - the courgettes will go a delicate shade of yellow.

4 Cut the beef in strips, sear briefly in hot oil, season lightly and add to the hot sauce. Bring back to a boil and season to taste. Garnish the meat with the courgette strips.

Marinated Fillet of Beef
in a Spicy Sauce

Recipe by Rolf von Siebenthal

Noisettes of Lamb with a Peanut Sauce

Recipe by Rolf von Siebenthal

8 noisettes of lamb, each about 50g
salt and freshly ground pepper
a little oil for frying

1 shallot, finely chopped
2 cloves garlic, mashed
a little finely chopped fresh chili, seeded
if wished
a little lemongrass, finely sliced
1 tbsp oil
25g chilli paste
75g roasted peanuts
300ml water
1 tsp sugar

1 Soften the shallots, garlic, chillies and lemongrass in the oil, add the chilli paste and peanuts and cook together briefly. Moisten with the water, boil up briefly and blend till smooth in the liquidiser. Add the sugar, bring back to the boil and taste for seasoning.

2 Season the lamb and sear in hot oil for 3–4 minutes until crusty but still nicely pink inside. Serve with the sauce.

Coconut Torte with Mango

Recipe by Rolf von Siebenthal

For a 16cm-diameter cake tin, 3cm deep

150g shortcrust pastry (see recipe
page 193)
dried beans or cherry stones for baking
blind

75g fresh mango, cut in cubes
150ml milk
1 egg, separated
1 tbsp cornflour
2 tbsp whipping cream
2 tbsp caster sugar
150g coconut flakes
100g brown sugar
1 tbsp water
1 tbsp plain white flour

1 Heat the oven to 200ºC/Gas 6 and lightly butter the cake tin. Roll out the pastry fairly thickly and use it to line the tin. Prick the bottom with a fork. Lay a piece of greaseproof paper in it and fill with dried beans or cherry stones. Bake the pastry blind for 10 minutes or until just set. Let it cool a little and remove the paper and beans or stones. Reduce the oven heat to 180ºC/Gas 4.

2 Scatter the mango cubes in the bottom of the pastry. Mix the cornflour with a little milk and the egg yolk until smooth. Put the rest of the milk in a saucepan with the cream and caster sugar and bring to a boil. Stir in the cornflour mixture and bring back to the boil. Add 50g of the coconut flakes, mix well and pour over the mango cubes.

3 Beat the egg whites with a level tablespoon of the brown sugar to a firm snow. Dissolve the rest of the sugar in the water and fold it carefully into the egg whites. Fold in the remaining coconut flakes and the flour. Pipe or spoon the mixture over the cake. Bake for 25-30 minutes.

Indian-Style Jellied Almond Creams

Recipe by Rolf von Siebenthal

350ml milk
35g brown sugar
a pinch of saffron
a pinch of powdered cardamom
a pinch of agar-agar
½ carrot, finely grated
3 tbsp ground almonds
2 tbsp sultanas

200g natural yogurt
grilled flaked almonds

1 Bring the milk to a boil with the sugar, saffron, cardamom and agar-agar. Add the carrot, almonds and sultanas, boil again and simmer for 3–4 minutes. Cool for about 5 minutes, pour into 4 timbale moulds or coffee cups and chill for 12 hours.

2 Spread some yogurt onto the plates, turn the creams out on top. Sprinkle with grilled flaked almonds.

Mediterranean
Holidays Culinary yearnings for
those who stayed at home

It's good
   to be here again.

Do you still remember the bar
we fled to to escape from a summer
thunderstorm?

How the rain wouldn't stop and we breathlessly
drank to celebrate our good fortune?

You always loved thunderstorms,
the intensity and suddenness that
changes everything.

Do you sometimes think of that haggard little man who ate a
sandwich every day for lunch that was almost as big as he was?

Of Tonino and old Monsieur Gérard?

If you were here now,
we would always sit at the
         same table, and I would
have to win it back
     for you if it was
         already occupied.

You need a familiar place, you told me,
in order to risk everything without reservation —
              the moment, love, silence,
light and darkness.

100

risk everything

without reser-

vation –

the moment,

love, silence,

light and

darkness.   I am drinking our wine and feeding the pigeons.

                              Do you think they could be the same ones?

                    How old do pigeons get?

you fly

with your

nose back

to the

source of

a scent

If you were here now, we would only
read newspapers in languages we don't understand.
We would make up news
and stories and believe they were true.
We would waste time without losing it.

We would roam over
the fields in the early
morning and along the beach at night,
to seek out new smells.

You told me that you were a "nose fairy,"
that you fly with your nose back to the source
of a scent — and you squeezed your eyes shut
tight when you discovered a smell that you
couldn't identify.
You breathed in the smell deeply until it
belonged only to you.
Those are my photographs, you said.

Now I am smelling the musty cool of the stone wall
and the heat of the dust, and I am drinking our wine.

I wonder if the pigeons would
remember you if you were here?

Spaghetti with Mascarpone and Caviar

Recipe by Rolf von Siebenthal

100ml light veal stock (see recipe page 192)
200ml whipping cream
250g Mascarpone
a pinch of agar-agar
25g grated Parmesan
salt and freshly ground pepper

300g medium-fine spaghetti
100g ossetra caviar

1 Boil the stock with the cream until reduced by half. Whisk in the Mascarpone and bring back briefly to a simmer. Remove from the heat, add the agar-agar and stir well. Add the Parmesan and season to taste.

2 Cook the spaghetti in boiling salted water until al dente. Drain well, add it to the sauce and mix well.

3 Serve the spaghetti in soup bowls and top each serving with a little mound of caviar.

Gazpacho

Recipe by Rolf von Siebenthal

800g tomatoes, peeled and seeded
½ a red pepper, seeds removed
175g cucumbers, halved and seeded
100ml light veal stock (see recipe page 192)
3 tbsp red wine
a sprig of basil
salt and freshly ground pepper
Tabasco sauce

Garnishes:
croutons
diced yellow and green pepper
4 fine basil leaves

1 Blend together all the ingredients for the gazpacho in a liquidiser or food processor until smooth. Push through a sieve and season quite highly with the salt, pepper and Tabasco. Chill well.

2 Serve the soup sprinkled with croutons and pepper cubes and garnished with some basil leaves.

Couscous Salad

Recipe by Rolf von Siebenthal

300ml light veal stock (see recipe page 192)
2 tbsp lemon juice
1 shallot, finely chopped
150g couscous

a 100g piece of boned rack of lamb
oil for frying
salt and freshly ground pepper

50g shiitake mushrooms, sliced
15g butter
a handful of mangetout (sugar snap peas), cut in strips
¼ of a yellow and red pepper, cut in strips
2 tbsp herb vinegar
4 tbsp safflower oil
2 sprigs fresh coriander, roughly chopped

1 Bring the stock to a boil with the lemon juice and shallot. Stir in the couscous, bring back to the boil, cover and leave to steep for 5 minutes. Drain.

2 Season the lamb and sear in a little oil on all sides. It should remain pink inside. Cool and slice thinly.

3 Stew the mushrooms gently in the butter. Blanch the mangetout and pepper strips.

4 Mix everything together carefully, season with the oil, vinegar, salt and pepper. Sprinkle the coriander on top of the salad.

Tip:
To make it easier to peel tomatoes, cut away the core and cut a cross in the skin. Put them in boiling water, drain and refresh in cold water. To seed the tomatoes, cut them in half and squeeze out the seeds.

Crostini

Recipe by Rolf von Siebenthal

Olive crostini:
4 thin slices baguette
25g green olives, stoned, finely chopped
25g Mascarpone
a little chives, finely chopped
salt and freshly ground pepper

Anchovy crostini:
4 thin slices baguette
25g anchovy fillets, finely chopped
25g Mascarpone
a little chopped parsley

Tomato crostini:
4 thin slices baguette
½ clove garlic, mashed
50g tomato confit (see recipe page 107)
4 small basil leaves

Veal Ravioli with Spinach and Pesto

Recipe by Roland Jöhri

1 Toast the baguette slices. Rub the garlic into 4 of the slices for the tomato crostini. Mix together the other ingredients for each topping and spread onto the toasted slices. Garnish with the herbs.

Serves about 10	**250g spinach, trimmed, washed and drained**
Pasta dough:	**salt and freshly ground pepper, nutmeg**
6 eggs	
1 tbsp oil	**a handful each of breadcrumbs and Parmesan**
a little water	
salt	**25g butter, heated till nut-brown and cooled**
500g strong white bread flour	**1–2 eggs**
Filling:	
½ an onion	**Pesto:**
1 clove garlic	**1 clove garlic**
rosemary, marjoram, thyme	**½ bunch basil**
	100ml cold-pressed olive oil
250g each pork and veal	
150g calves sweetbreads, raw	**200g spinach**

Tip:
It's a good idea to make the full quantity, even if it seems rather a lot. The ravioli can be frozen raw.

1 To make the pasta dough, beat together the eggs, oil, water and salt in the electric mixer until foaming. (You should have about 250ml altogether.) Mix in the flour. Knead thoroughly until smooth, firm and elastic. Form the dough into 4 rolls, wrap them in clingfilm and refrigerate overnight. Cut the dough in thin slices, and roll them out in a pasta machine, working up gradually to the finest setting. Two pairs of hands are a great help for this operation.

2 For the filling, soften the onion and garlic in the butter with the herbs. Put the meat, sweetbreads and spinach through the mincer using the finest blade or process finely in a food processor. Season with salt, pepper and nutmeg. Add the

Basil Gnocchi with Tomato Confit

Recipe by Rolf von Siebenthal

600g floury potatoes
a good handful of fresh basil leaves
1 tbsp olive oil
2 eggs
100g plain white flour
salt and freshly ground pepper
nutmeg

Tomato Confit:
1 shallot, finely chopped
1 clove garlic, mashed
2 tbsp tomato purée
2 tbsp olive oil
fresh oregano, thyme and marjoram, finely chopped
500g tomatoes, peeled, seeded and finely chopped
salt and freshly ground pepper
nutmeg

50g grated Parmesan
4 fine basil leaves

1 Cook the potatoes in their skins. Peel while still hot, mash them and allow to cool a little. Chop the basil finely and mix with the olive oil. Stir it into the eggs and add to the potato purée. Mix in the flour, season with salt, pepper and nutmeg. Form into gnocchi and press with a fork. Bring a large pan of salted water to a boil and add a splash of oil. Poach the gnocchi until they float to the top, lift out with a slotted spoon and drain well.

remaining ingredients and mix together well. If necessary, adjust the seasoning and chill the filling thoroughly. Pipe or spoon small blobs of filling onto the ravioli sheets, cover with more ravioli sheets and press the edges together to seal.

3 For the pesto, chop the garlic and basil together finely and mix them with the olive oil.

4 Cook the ravioli for 2–3 minutes in boiling salted water. Cook the spinach gently in a little butter, add the ravioli to the pan and cook together briefly. Stir in the pesto and arrange on heated plates.

2 For the tomato confit, heat the oil and sweat the shallot, garlic and tomato purée briefly in it. Add the chopped herbs and tomatoes. Bubble up and cook gently for a minute or two. Season to taste.

3 Spoon the hot tomato confit onto plates, arrange the gnocchi on top, sprinkle with grated Parmesan and garnish with a basil leaf.

4 thick slices monkfish on the bone, each about 150g

coarse salt and freshly ground pepper

olive oil

Herby Polenta:

200g fine polenta flour

800ml chicken stock

1 tbsp mixed herbs (basil, marjoram, parsley), chopped and steeped in olive oil

Barolo Sauce:

2 shallots, thinly sliced

2 lumps brown sugar

300ml Barolo (or other full-bodied red wine)

50g chilled butter, cubed

1 Cook the polenta with the stock over gentle heat for about 30 minutes or according to the package instructions till soft. Stir in the herbs and season with salt and pepper. Keep it warm.

2 For the sauce, cook the shallots in a little butter with the sugar lumps until lightly caramelised. Add the wine and cook it down slowly to a quarter of its volume. Strain the contents of the pan and then whisk in the cold butter.

3 Season the monkfish, sear in hot oil until just cooked and allow to stand for a few minutes.

4 Arrange the cooked polenta in a circle on the plate. Put the monkfish on top and pour over the sauce. A good garnish would be some fanned-out slices of fried aubergine.

Monkfish with Herby Polenta and Barolo Sauce

Recipe by Roland Jöhri

Tip: Provençal Vegetables also go very well with this dish (see recipe page 109).

3 Process the vegetables roughly in a food processor, or chop them roughly and stir in the parsley.

4 Butter the baking rings and put them on a baking sheet lined with non-stick baking paper. Layer the lasagne sheets with the vegetable mixture, starting and finishing with a lasagne sheet. Spoon a tablespoon of Béchamel sauce on top of each one, sprinkle with Parmesan and dot with butter.

5 Heat the oven to 200°C/Gas 6. Bake the lasagnes for 10–12 minutes or until nicely brown on top and hot through. Lift the lasagnes in their rings using a fish slice and place them on heated plates. Sprinkle with a little olive oil.

Vegetable Lasagne with Ceps
Recipe by Wolfgang Kuchler

For 4 bottomless baking rings each about 12–15cm in diameter

200g pasta dough (see recipe page 192)

250g vegetables in season (spring onions, celery, carrots, kohlrabi, leeks, courgettes etc.), trimmed, neatly and evenly sliced
50g fresh ceps, sliced
4 tbsp extra-virgin olive oil
4 tbsp vegetable stock
3 tbsp whipping cream
2 tbsp finely chopped flat-leaved parsley
salt and freshly ground pepper
nutmeg, curry powder

Béchamel Sauce:
200ml milk
10g soft butter
1 tbsp plain white flour
1 tbsp whipping cream
salt and freshly ground pepper
nutmeg

grated Parmesan
butter dots

1 Roll out the pasta dough thinly and cut into 20 circles each about 12–15cm in diameter.

2 Sweat the vegetables together with the ceps in the oil. Season, moisten with the stock and cream and continue cooking till barely tender. They should remain a little crunchy. Cook the lasagne rounds in plenty of boiling salted water until al dente. Drain.

Provençal Vegetables
Recipe by Roland Jöhri

1 tomato
1 courgette
1 aubergine
1 red pepper
1 yellow pepper
olive oil
½ clove of garlic, mashed
finely snipped basil
sea salt and freshly ground pepper

1 Peel the vegetables and cut in 1cm cubes. Sweat them gently in hot olive oil, add the garlic and cook until the vegetables are barely tender. Sprinkle with basil and season to taste.

Merlot Risotto with Gorgonzola

Recipe by Wolfgang Kuchler

50g finely diced onions

25g butter

2 tbsp extra-virgin olive oil

200g risotto rice

400ml Merlot, or better still, Pomerol with a high Merlot content

500–600ml light chicken stock

50g Gorgonzola

50ml whipping cream

2 tbsp finely chopped rocket leaves

1–2 lobster shells

50g butter

1 shallot, finely chopped

¼ clove garlic, finely chopped

2 tbsp Cognac

100ml dry white wine

2 small tomatoes, peeled, seeded and diced

1 tbsp tomato puree

350ml fish stock

10 threads of saffron

thyme, bay leaf, peppercorns, parsley, dill sprigs

250ml whipping cream

2 tbsp white vermouth

1 tbsp port

50g monkfish on the bone

50g each salmon and sole fillets

2 scampi

2 prawns

3 tbsp olive oil

1 small cooked lobster, about 400g, shelled

4 mussels, cleaned

a little celeriac and onion, finely chopped

100ml white wine

fennel or courgette, optional, blanched

sea salt and freshly ground pepper

1 Soften the onions in the oil and butter without allowing them to brown. Add the rice, stir well. Moisten with the wine and allow the wine to reduce to almost nothing. Bring the stock to a boil in a separate saucepan and add it to the rice. Cook, stirring constantly, until the risotto is al dente. Stir in the Gorgonzola, cream and rocket, bring back to the boil and serve at once.

Tip:
In order to give the risotto an even deeper red colour, stir in 2 tablespoons beetroot juice just at the end. A saffron risotto can be prepared in the same way, but instead of Merlot use Chardonnay in which you have dissolved a good pinch of powdered saffron or some saffron threads. Finish with Parmesan instead of Gorgonzola, and stir in a little cream. If wished, finely diced tomato can be added at the end.

Garlic Bread

Recipe by Roland Jöhri

1 small baguette

50g soft butter

thyme, dill, chervil, flat-leaved parsley

3 cloves garlic, mashed

salt and freshly ground pepper, Tabasco

1 Let the butter stand at room temperature overnight, so that it is easy to work with. Wash the herbs, shake dry and chop them finely with a sharp knife. Work them evenly into the butter. Add the garlic and season with salt and pepper. (The garlic butter also freezes well. Form into cylinders and wrap in greaseproof paper.)

2 Cut the bread in slices. Film a pan with olive oil and fry the slices on both sides till golden brown and crusty. Spread the slices with garlic butter and bake them briefly in a hot oven until the butter melts.

Bouillabaisse

Recipe by Roland Jöhri

1 Chop up the lobster shells and fry them gently in the butter. Add the shallot and garlic and cook a little more. Moisten with the Cognac and white wine and simmer gently. Add the tomato dice and purée. Cook over gentle heat, add the stock, saffron threads, herbs and cream and cook the soup till lightly thickened. Put in a sieve lined with muslin held over a bowl, press out all the juice. Add the vermouth and port, season and whisk together briefly.

2 If possible, buy the fish and shellfish ready trimmed. Cut in pieces so as to give four good servings. Fry the fish pieces and the prawns and scampi in some of the hot oil, season. Keep them warm. Put the lobster on a baking sheet, sprinkle with a little salted water, cover with foil and heat it through for a few minutes at 80°C (no hotter, otherwise the lobster will toughen). Sweat the mussels with the celeriac and onions in a little olive oil. Moisten with the wine, cover the pan and cook until they open – just a few minutes. Lift out the mussel flesh and add to the bouillabaisse.

3 Arrange the fish, shellfish and blanched fennel or courgette (if used) in soup plates and spoon the hot bouillabaisse over.

Tip:
Garlic bread (see recipe page 110) and garlic sauce can also be served.

111

Paella

Recipe by Roland Jöhri

1 Fry the chicken pieces in hot oil. Add the shallot, garlic and squid to the pan. Dissolve the saffron in ½ litre of the stock and add to the pan with the rice. Cook gently, gradually adding the diced pepper, courgettes and peas. Add the chopped

2 chicken legs (thigh with drumstick), each cut in 2 pieces
100ml olive oil
1 shallot, finely chopped
1 clove garlic, finely chopped
100g baby squid
300g risotto rice
1 tsp powdered saffron
¾ litre chicken stock
50g red pepper, diced
50g courgettes, sliced
50g peas
1 tbsp chopped herbs
olive oil
salt and freshly ground pepper

about 800g fillet of turbot, monkfish, salmon, sole and John Dory
4 scampi
4 giant prawns
1 lobster (about 600g)
1kg (weight in the shell) clams, cockles, mussels, New Zealand green mussels and scallops
parsley and dill, chopped

herbs. Pour in the remaining stock and cook till just al dente. Season with salt, pepper and olive oil.

2 Prepare the fish and shellfish. Clean the shellfish and mussels thoroughly and cook in fish stock for a few minutes or until the mussels open. Discard any which do not open. Season the fish and fry briefly in butter.

3 Put the rice on a serving dish and arrange the fish and shellfish on top. Sprinkle with the chopped dill and parsley and drizzle olive oil on top.

Rum Babas with Grapes and Sabayon

Recipe by Roland Jöhri

For 8–10 mini rum baba moulds about 8cm in diameter

Savarin dough:	Syrup for soaking the rum babas:
220g plain white flour	350ml water
125ml milk	325g caster sugar
15g yeast	175ml rum
80g butter	juice of 1 orange
1 tbsp caster sugar	
2–3 egg yolks	Sabayon:
a small pinch of vanilla sugar	3 egg yolks
a little lemon juice	250ml Sauternes
	2 tbsp vanilla sugar
	grated zest of 1 lemon

400g grapes

Tip:
If all the babas are not used, stored them in a cool place and soak in syrup only just before using.

1 Mix together 120g flour with the milk and crumbled yeast and allow to rise for 15–20 minutes in a warm place. Beat the butter and sugar together until pale and fluffy. Beat in the egg yolks alternately with a bit more flour. Finally, add the yeast mixture, the rest of the flour, the vanilla sugar and lemon juice. Grease and flour the baba moulds, arrange the dough in them and allow to rise again briefly. Heat the oven to 200°C/Gas 6. Bake the babas for about 10 minutes. Allow them to cool thoroughly.

2 Mix together all the ingredients for the soaking syrup and heat them. Soak the cooled babas thoroughly in the syrup.

3 Peel and seed the grapes.

4 For the sabayon, put the egg yolks with the Sauternes, vanilla sugar and grated lemon zest in a bowl set over boiling water and beat until foaming. Continue beating over iced water until thick and creamy. Serve with the warm babas, together with the grapes.

Ohm Ali
Recipe by Beat Gehrig

For 4 ramekins

**50g puff pastry
or 2 vol-au-vent cases
25g coconut flakes
50g almonds, blanched and chopped
50g sultanas
50g pistachio nuts, peeled and chopped
325ml milk
125g honey
1 egg white
50g brown sugar
a few pistachio nuts to decorate, blanched
and chopped**

1 Roll out the puff pastry thinly (the size is immaterial), place on a buttered baking sheet, prick with a fork and leave to rest for 3 hours in a cool place. Heat the oven to 180°C/Gas 4. Bake the pastry for about 20 minutes. Cool.

2 Crumble the baked pastry (or vol-au-vent cases) into small pieces and divide between the soufflé dishes. Divide the coconut flakes, almonds, sultanas and pistachio nuts evenly between the dishes.

3 Put the milk and honey in a pan and bring to a boil. Pour some of it into the soufflé dishes and leave for 2 hours. When the mixture has thickened a little, add more of the honey-milk mixture.

4 Heat the oven to 170°C/Gas 3. Beat the egg whites with the sugar until stiff and pipe on top of the dishes using a piping bag. Bake the soufflés for 25 minutes. Remove from the oven and sprinkle with the pistachio nuts. Serve at once, before the soufflés collapse.

Orange Torte with Quark
Recipe by Rolf von Siebenthal

**100g shortcrust pastry (see recipe
page 193)**

**150g quark or *fromage frais*
2 tbsp caster sugar
4 tbsp orange juice
1 tbsp lemon juice
5g agar-agar
150ml whipping cream
4 tbsp apricot jam, sieved
strips of orange zest to garnish**

1 Heat the oven to 170°C/Gas 3. Roll out the pastry thinly, cut a disc 16cm in diameter, place on a buttered baking sheet, prick all over with a fork and bake for 10–15 minutes.

2 Mix the quark or *fromage frais* with the sugar. Boil the orange juice, lemon juice and agar-agar together and mix into the quark or *fromage frais*. Cool to about 30°C. Whip the cream till it forms soft peaks and fold it carefully into the mixture.

3 Lay the pastry in the bottom of a 16cm-diameter cake ring or springform tin, fill with the quark mixture and smooth the top with a palette knife. Freeze until set.

4 Heat the apricot jam and brush it in a thin glaze over the tart. Remove the ring or release the springform, garnish the tart with orange zests and serve.

**Tip:
It is easiest
to slice the
tart when
still half-
frozen.**

114

Noah's Ark

A DAY OFF FOR ANIMALS

AND THEY ALL CAME TOGETHER IN ONE PLACE

Check-in for animals – on the way to a vegetarian
paradise, where animals can enjoy a day off.
And humans are content without meat. For example,
with recipes that make not only confirmed
vegetarians hungry as a bear.

Carpaccio of Bergell Dumplings with a Salad of Raw Asparagus

Recipe by Roland Jöhri

Bergell Dumplings:
100g white bread, cut in cubes
100g bread rolls, cut in cubes
salt and freshly ground pepper, nutmeg
a little chopped parsley and chives
1 shallot, finely chopped
a knob of butter
200ml milk
3 eggs, separated

Asparagus salad:
325g green asparagus, trimmed
coarse salt and freshly ground pepper
lemon juice, sugar
4–5 tbsp sherry dressing (see recipe page 191)

Tip:
The dumpling recipe seems very large, but it does not work well with a smaller quantity. Any leftovers can be used as an accompaniment for meat dishes. In this case, slice the chilled dumplings and fry gently in butter on both sides.

1 In a bowl, mix together the bread cubes, salt, pepper, nutmeg, parsley and chives. Soften the shallots in the butter, add the milk and heat gently. Stir in the egg yolks, and pour this mixture over the bread in the bowl. Leave in a cool place for the bread to soak up the liquid. Beat the egg whites and fold them in carefully.

2 Roll the mixture into cylinder-shaped dumplings and place on a buttered sheet of foil as they are ready. Bring a large pan of water to a bare simmer (it should not boil) and poach the dumplings gently for 30 minutes. Remove and allow them to cool on a tray.

3 Meanwhile make the asparagus salad. Cut off the tips and use them to garnish the dish. Slice the stalks very thinly, using a mandoline slicer or potato peeler. Sprinkle with coarse salt, pepper, lemon juice, sugar and 4–5 tbsp sherry dressing and leave to marinate briefly.

4 Slice the chilled dumplings very thinly and arrange on plates. Brush generously with some dressing and sprinkle more dressing over the dumpling slices just before serving.

Tagliolini with Carrot Sauce, Fresh Garden Peas and Mint

Recipe by Wolfgang Kuchler

1 litre carrot juice (preferably home-made)
100ml Sauternes
200ml Italian Chardonnay (or other dry white wine)
50g butter, chilled
300g pasta dough (see recipe page 192)
20 mint leaves, finely shredded
4 tbsp olive oil
125g shelled peas, blanched
sea salt
a little olive oil

1 Put the carrot juice, Sauternes and Chardonnay in a large saucepan and boil down hard to reduce to about 400ml. Whisk in the chilled butter and keep the sauce warm.

2 Roll out the pasta dough thinly and cut fine noodles from it. Cook until al dente in plenty of boiling salted water. Drain and immediately drop them into the pan with the carrot sauce. Stir until thoroughly coated. Heat some of the mint leaves in the olive oil and mix them with the blanched peas. Season.

3 Arrange the noodles in soup bowls and divide the peas between them. Garnish with more mint leaves, sprinkle with a little olive oil and serve at once.

Yogurt Terrine with Chives

Recipe by Rolf von Siebenthal

For a 1-litre terrine

200ml water
200ml whipping cream
10g agar-agar
400ml natural yogurt
4 bunches chives, finely chopped
salt and freshly ground pepper

1 Put the water, cream and agar-agar in a small saucepan and bring to a boil. Remove from the heat and allow to cool.

2 Stir in the yogurt and chives. Season with salt and pepper, pour into the terrine and chill for several hours or until set.

Ricotta and Spinach Beet Roulade with Tomato Vinaigrette

Recipe by Wolfgang Kuchler

10 leaves spinach beet, or chard or spinach

250g firm ricotta

1 tbsp extra-virgin olive oil

1 large tomato, peeled, seeded and diced

2 courgettes, sliced thinly

4 tbsp olive oil vinaigrette (see recipe page 191)

a bunch of chives, chopped

salt and freshly ground pepper

1 Blanch the beet, chard or spinach leaves, drain and lay them on a sheet of clingfilm to form a rectangle. Slice the ricotta and lay the slices in a long strip on top of the leaves. Season, sprinkle with olive oil. Roll the whole thing up firmly in the clingfilm and chill.

2 Stew the tomato dice in a little olive oil until somewhat thickened. Blanch the courgette slices, drain and pat them dry on paper towels. Arrange them in circles on serving plates, top with some of the diced tomato and finish each serving with a 3 cm slice of roulade. Sprinkle with chives and drizzle some olive oil vinaigrette over the courgette slices.

Green Asparagus Chartreuses

Recipe by Wolfgang Kuchler

For 4 bottomless rings each about 6–7cm
in diameter

400g green asparagus, trimmed
a pinch of sugar
butter
200g potato purée (see recipe page 58)
8 tbsp parsley *jus* (see recipe below)
olive oil
salt and freshly ground pepper

1 Cook the asparagus in boiling salted water with a pinch of sugar and a knob of butter for 3–5 minutes or until just tender. Cut the top 5–6 cm off the asparagus stalks. Reserve the tips and cut the stalks in small cubes.

2 Butter the rings and set them on a sheet of baking paper. Line with the asparagus tips, standing them up all around the inside. Fill with the potato purée. Heat the asparagus cubes in a little butter, season and add to the purée in the ring moulds.

3 Place each ring mould in the middle of the plate using a fish slice and slide the paper out from beneath it. Lift off the rings. Pour the parsley *jus* over and serve at once.

Tip:
If you don't have small baking rings, use tuna cans from which you have removed the top and bottom; or simply arrange the asparagus fanned out on top of each serving of purée and pour the sauce over.

Parsley Jus

Recipe by Wolfgang Kuchler

Gives about 200ml *jus*

100g parsley leaves (weight without stalks)
2 tbsp extra-virgin olive oil
100ml light chicken stock
100ml whipping cream
salt and freshly ground pepper, nutmeg
white Balsamic vinegar

1 Sweat the parsley leaves briefly in the olive oil, moisten with the stock, add the cream and bring to a boil. Season with salt, pepper and nutmeg, blend until smooth in a liquidiser and strain. Sharpen with a little Balsamic vinegar.

Pizokel with cabbage
Recipe by Roland Jöhri

150g low-fat quark or *fromage frais*
2 eggs
1 egg yolk
salt and freshly ground pepper, nutmeg
125g plain white flour

200g Savoy cabbage
a little butter
½ clove garlic, finely chopped
1 shallot, chopped
4 tbsp vegetable stock
125ml whipped cream
salt and freshly ground pepper, nutmeg

1 Beat together the quark or *fromage frais*, eggs and egg yolk in a bowl. Season with salt, pepper and nutmeg. Work in the flour to make a batter. Spread some of this batter onto a small chopping board and slice ribbons of it off the edge of the board (as for *Spätzle*) directly into boiling salted water. Lift out the *Pizokel* with a slotted spoon as they float to the surface and drain them.

2 Shred the cabbage fairly thickly and blanch in boiling salted water. Drain well. Heat the butter in a frying pan and soften the garlic, shallot and cabbage. Moisten with vegetable stock, cook for a while and then stir in the *Pizokel*. Season to taste and stir in the cream before serving.

Tip:
Pizokel can also be served as a main course, in which case they are nice mixed with some sautéd mushrooms.

Many recipes call for a **mixture of butter and olive oil** for frying. For this, you need roughly equal quantities of oil and butter. This gives a good, well-rounded flavour, and the mixture can be heated to a higher temperature with less danger of burning, since oil has a higher burning point than butter.

Fennel Piccata with Rocket Noodles and Tomato Sabayon
Recipe by Wolfgang Kuchler

4 fennel bulbs
2 eggs
50g each Parmesan and Pecorino, grated
plain white flour
25g butter
2 tbsp olive oil
salt and pepper

200g fine, rocket-flavoured noodles (made from pasta dough, recipe page 192, plus 2 tbsp rocket purée)

Tomato Sabayon:
100ml tomato juice
a splash of dry white vermouth
lemon juice
sea salt and freshly ground pepper
1 egg yolk

olive oil
1 medium tomato, peeled, seeded and diced

1 Cook the fennel until just tender in boiling, salted water. Drain, pat dry and cut into 12 slices about ½ cm thick. Beat the eggs together with the Parmesan and Pecorino. Season the fennel slices lightly and dust them with flour. Dip them in the egg and cheese mixture until well coated. Heat the olive oil and the butter and fry the slices until golden brown.

2 Cook the noodles in boiling salted water until al dente.

3 For the sabayon, put all the ingredients together in a bowl and beat over simmering water until thick and foaming. Drain the noodles and arrange them on heated plates. Lay the fennel slices on top and spoon the sabayon around. Garnish with tomato cubes and drizzle some olive oil over.

150g strudel pastry (see recipe page 193)

1 large tomato
200g leeks, cleaned
200g bean sprouts
1 shallot, chopped
2 cloves garlic, mashed
25g butter
35g semolina
100ml whipping cream
salt and freshly ground pepper

1 egg, mixed with a fork
15g melted butter

Pepper Sauce:
300g red peppers
a knob of butter
100ml white wine
100ml vegetable stock
100ml whipping cream

Leek and Bean Sprout Strudel with Red Pepper Sauce

Recipe by Rolf von Siebenthal

1 Plunge the tomato in boiling water, remove the skin, cut in half and squeeze out the seeds. Cut in lozenge-shaped pieces. Cut the leek in strips about 5 x ½ cm. Blanch the leek strips and bean sprouts separately.

2 Soften the shallot and garlic in the butter, add the leeks and bean sprouts, cook together briefly. Sprinkle in the semolina, stirring to mix well. Add the cream and bring to a boil, stirring constantly. Season to taste, cool.

3 Cut a piece of clingfilm 30x35cm. Roll out the strudel pastry very thinly to the same size as the clingfilm and lay it on top. Arrange the cooled vegetables on the pastry, add the tomato lozenges and roll up the strudel carefully using the clingfilm to help you. Put it on a baking sheet lined with non-stick baking paper and leave to rest for 1 hour in a cool place.

4 Heat the oven to 200ºC/Gas 6. Brush the strudel with egg and bake for 30 minutes. Remove from the oven and brush with melted butter.

5 Meanwhile make the pepper sauce: roast or grill the peppers until thoroughly blistered, wrap in a teatowel and allow to cool a little. Rub off the skin under running water and remove the cores and seeds. Cut the flesh in small pieces and soften them in a little butter. Moisten with the white wine and stock and cook briefly. Blend until smooth in the liquidiser or food processor, push through a sieve. Put back in the pan, add the cream and bring to a boil again. Simmer gently until the sauce is lightly thickened. Season to taste.

Onion Compote with Saffron
Recipe by Rolf von Siebenthal

200g onions, peeled
a knob of butter
1 pinch of saffron
2 tbsp white wine
salt and freshly ground pepper

1 Slice the onions evenly, blanch, drain and cool them. Soften them in the hot butter, sprinkle the saffron over and season with salt and pepper. Add the wine, cook together briefly and check the seasoning.

Lentil Burgers with Curry Sauce

Recipe by Rolf von Siebenthal

Makes 8 burgers

50g brown lentils
200g potatoes
1 small shallot, finely chopped
1 clove garlic, mashed
a knob of butter
a little carrot and celeriac, finely diced
5 sprigs parsley, chopped
2 tbsp curry powder
2 eggs, separated
salt and freshly ground pepper

Curry Sauce:
1 shallot, finely chopped
2 cloves garlic, mashed
a knob of butter
½ an apple
a slice of pineapple, fresh or tinned
½ a banana
100ml white wine
100ml vegetable stock
2 tsp curry powder
½ tbsp tomato purée
2 tbsp whipped cream

a little plain white flour
50g sesame seeds
50g butter for frying

1 Soak the lentils in warm water for a while. Drain, put them in a pan with fresh water to cover and cook for 8–12 minutes till tender. Boil the potatoes in their skins.

2 Soften the shallot and garlic in the butter, add the vegetables and cook together briefly. Add the drained lentils, parsley and curry powder, mixing well.

3 Peel the potatoes and mash them. Add the egg yolks and the lentil mixture, mix well and season to taste. Place the mixture between two sheets of clingfilm and roll it out about 1.5 cm thick. Stamp out burgers each about 4.5 cm in diameter.

4 For the curry sauce, soften the shallot and garlic in the butter. Chop all the fruit roughly and add it to the pan. Moisten with the wine and stock and bring to a boil. Blend in the liquidiser or food processor until smooth. Bring back to a boil, add the curry powder and tomato purée and let the sauce reduce a bit. Shortly before serving, whisk in the whipped cream.

5 Dust the burgers lightly in flour, dip in the egg whites and then in the sesame seeds. Fry till golden brown in hot butter.

Cabbage and Sweetcorn

Recipe by Rolf von Siebenthal

150g Savoy cabbage, cut in little squares
1 shallot, chopped
a knob of butter
200ml whipping cream
75g sweetcorn
salt and freshly ground pepper
a little nutmeg

1 Blanch the cabbage, drain and refresh in cold water. Soften the shallot in the butter, add the cabbage and cook together. Pour in the cream, season with salt, pepper and nutmeg and cook until reduced by about half. Stir in the sweetcorn and check the seasoning.

GUEST DIARY

COMMENTS

27.8.98

Jackie / Mike   crostini

No tomatoes for Jackie –
next time Chardonnay for Mike!

COMMENTS

The three flowers or: Why the people of the Engadine greet each other with "Allegra!"

It happened once upon a time, long, long ago, when life in the high valley today known as the Engadine was still harsh and impoverished. Summers were short, winters long and icy, and provisions never lasted long enough. Melancholy, sickness and death settled over the valley. A flower angel heard the moaning and crying and took pity. He slipped into the guise of a beautiful girl with golden curls, knocked on the door of the desperate people and spoke: "I am Flurina, and I want to help you. Look, I give you the seeds of three magic flowers: the yellow flower will guard you against hunger, the red one against the cold, and the blue one against gloom. Sow them, and look after them well." Soon yellow, red and blue flowers were blooming everywhere. The winter returned with all its fury, and as the flower angel had told them, the people laid a red seed in all the rooms and behold, it was always comfortably warm. Although the days were dark and short, the people laughed and sang and joked, because each of them wore a blue seed around their neck. And when the provisions began to run out, they ate a seed of the yellow flower, and their hunger was stilled. It could have gone on like this for an eternity, if a person could stand so much good fortune! But the people began to be careless and lazy, because the seeds took care of their every need – for warmth, for a full stomach, for happiness. Everything revolved around the three flowers, which they named Allegria, Pigna and Vivanda*. In time, however, the seeds were no longer planted lovingly and cultivated, but rather shamefully traded, stolen, and sold off. The flower angel looked down on all of this with sadness. He again took on the form of Flurina and knocked at the people's doors, and scolded them: "Now you will have to work hard again. You have not proven yourselves worthy of the magic flowers. Prepare yourselves for the winter!" The next day, the people saw with horror and fear that the flowers had dried up, and between Piz Saluver and Piz Padella, three rocky cliffs had ominously appeared overnight. An icy wind blew down from them and whispered, hissing, in their ears: "Allegria, Pigna, Vivanda!" Now the people knew that it was an exhortation. They quickly set to work, but it was too late. The winter came before they could harvest anything. Hunger and death were all around. After the snow melted, the survivors wrested a meagre harvest from the earth with grim determination. There was no time for laughter and jokes, there was only hardship and toiling. But as sparse as the harvest was, it helped them get through the next winter. Now the people had proved that they could manage to have firewood and full stomachs even without Pigna and Vivanda, and they were proud of this. Still, they missed the flower Allegria, because it could not be replaced with hard work. And so it came to pass that the wish for more cheerfulness and joy became a word of greeting, and since then the people of the Engadine greet each other with a hearty "Allegra!" And making sure that the magic flowers and the dark times are never forgotten are the three rocky cliffs, which still carry the name "las trais fluors" (the three flowers).

*joy, stove, food

Condensed version. Source: Legends from the Engadine, 1984, Classen Verlag

Stopover.
The Magic of the Moment.
The Gift of Time.

Stop over for a few hours — at two

thousand metres above all worldly things,

as Nietzsche says, where the light

is transparent, glowing in all colours,

enveloping all contrasts, all cen—

ters between ice and southern

spheres: a stopover in the Engadine, the

fateful high plateau for philosophers and

artists — and for...

a very special place, closer to

heaven and closer to earth, and

maybe "beyond good and evil,"

who knows?

As we reached the summit, we stood there as if dazzled. Our childhood visions lay materialised before us. To one side, glaciers shimmered. Below us, torrential mountain streams cut through the wild, deep-green Engadine countryside. Then a mysterious-looking range of hills; and behind them mauve-coloured slopes that opened up and then closed again, in front of a very blue area, a shimmering road leading to Italy.

Marcel Proust, *Leibhaftige Gegenwart*

300g Appenzeller cheese
2 sticks of celery, trimmed
1 small red apple

2 tbsp herb vinegar
4 tbsp safflower oil
½ tsp mustard
a little roughly chopped parsley
salt and freshly ground pepper

1 Cut the cheese and celery in 4cm lengths. Quarter, core and slice the apple. Shake the remaining ingredients together vigorously to make a vinaigrette. Pour over the salad and allow to stand for a bit before serving.

Celery Salad with Appenzeller Cheese and Apples

Recipe by Rolf von Siebenthal

600g organic beef
(sirloin, fillet or entrecote)
1 gherkin, drained
50g capers, drained
2 anchovies, drained
1 small onion
a bunch of parsley
1 tbsp Dijon mustard (hot)
1 tbsp cold-pressed olive oil
2 egg yolks
2 tbsp tomato ketchup
1 tsp paprika
1 tbsp Cognac
1 tbsp lemon juice
salt and freshly ground pepper
Tabasco sauce, cayenne pepper

4 small wholewheat baguettes
butter, softened

Wholewheat Baguette filled with Beef Tartare

Recipe by Roland Jöhri

1 Mince the meat in a meat mincer using the second finest blade or process fairly finely in a food processor.

2 Chop together finely the gherkin, capers, anchovies, onion and parsley and mix thoroughly with the minced meat. Stir in the mustard, olive oil, egg yolks, ketchup, paprika, Cognac and lemon juice. Season quite highly with salt, pepper, Tabasco and cayenne.

3 Cut the ends off the baguettes and remove most of the crumb. Spread the inside with soft butter. Fill with the beef tartare, using a forcing bag with a large nozzle if wished. Wrap the bread in foil and chill for about 1 hour in the freezer to firm up the filling.

4 Slice the chilled bread in 1cm thick slices and serve.

Maize-fed Chicken with Morel Salad and Caper Mousseline

Recipe by Roland Jöhri

4 maize-fed chicken breasts with wing attached

coarse salt and freshly ground pepper

oil for frying

Caper Mousseline:

2 shallots, finely chopped

50g capers

50g leeks, white part only, cut in strips

1 tbsp olive oil

175ml chicken stock

3 tbsp sour cream

lemon juice to taste

a little whipped cream

1 tbsp chopped herbs (e.g. flat-leaved parsley, chervil, mint)

Morel Salad:

250g fresh morels, cleaned

2 tbsp olive oil

4–5 tbsp sherry dressing (see recipe page 191)

½ tbsp chopped parsley

capers, lime segments and zest and chervil to garnish

1 Season the chicken breasts and sear in hot oil until just cooked. Keep warm.

2 For the mousseline, soften the shallots with the capers and leeks in olive oil for a few minutes. Put 5 tablespoons of the chicken stock in a small pan and reduce by fast boiling to 1 tablespoon – it should be quite syrupy. Add this to the shallots, capers and leeks with the rest of the chicken stock and simmer for 10–15 minutes. Tip everything into the liquidiser and blend till smooth. Strain and stir in the sour cream, season to taste with salt, pepper and a little lemon juice. Finally, fold in the whipped cream and the herbs.

3 For the morel salad, fry the morels briefly in the hot oil, season to taste, add the sherry dressing and sprinkle with chopped parsley.

4 Cut the chicken in thin slices and arrange nicely on plates. Drizzle the herb and caper mousseline over the tips of the slices and add the morel salad. Garnish with capers, lime segments and zest and some sprigs of chervil.

Iced Cucumber Soup

Recipe by Rolf von Siebenthal

450g cucumbers, unpeeled, cut in half lengthwise, seeds removed

150ml light veal stock (see recipe page 192)

75g low-fat quark or *fromage frais*

100ml natural yogurt

150ml whipping cream + 3–4 tbsp

fresh dill, roughly chopped

salt, Tabasco sauce

12 cucumber balls, cut with a small melon baller

croutons made from brown bread

1 Chop the cucumbers roughly and put them in the liquidiser or food processor with the stock. Blend until smooth, strain. Add the quark or *fromage frais*, 150ml cream and dill. Season with salt and Tabasco.

2 Pour the soup into well chilled bowls. Whip the rest of the cream until it forms soft peaks. Garnish the soup with a little whipped cream, the cucumber balls and the croutons.

Veal Pâté with Cumberland Sauce

Recipe by Rolf von Siebenthal

Tip:
All soups and sauces to be served cold tend to taste a bit bland, so be sure to season the soup quite highly.

For a 26cm-long loaf tin

500g shoulder of veal
125g back fat
1 shallot, chopped
100g mushrooms, finely chopped
½ apple, sliced
butter
a little thyme, marjoram and oregano
2 tbsp dry white vermouth
2 tbsp port
2 tbsp Cognac
50g pistachio nuts, peeled
salt and freshly ground pepper

2 slices fillet of veal, each about 50g
a knob of butter and a little oil for frying
2 handfuls spinach leaves, blanched
700g rich shortcrust pastry with egg white
(see recipe page 193)
1 egg to glaze

Aspic Jelly:
½ litre water
35g aspic jelly crystals
2 tbs port

Cumberland Sauce:
zest of 1 orange and ½ lemon, cut in thin strips
1 tbsp caster sugar
3 tbsp orange juice
1 tbsp lemon juice
1 tbsp full-bodied red wine
2 tbsp port
1 tbsp redcurrant jelly
a pinch of English mustard powder
a little finely grated horseradish
cayenne pepper
25g cranberries

1 Mince the veal and back fat using the 3mm blade, or have the butcher do this for you.
2 Soften the shallot, mushrooms and apple in a little butter, add the herbs and spices, moisten with the vermouth, port and Cognac. Put in a food processor and process together until fairly smoothly. Chill. Mix with the veal and fat, add the pistachios and mix again thoroughly. Season.
3 Sear the veal fillets in a little hot butter and oil. Set them aside to cool, then roll them up in the spinach leaves.
4 Roll out the pastry fairly thickly to a large rectangle. Using the inverted loaf tin as a template, cut out a rectangle for the lid about 1cm larger than the top of the tin and set it aside.

Arrange the rest of the pastry in the buttered tin. It should be in one piece, with no holes, and it must be large enough to overhang the tin by about 2cm all round.
5 Put half the minced meat mixture into the tin, and bang the tin down on the working surface to settle the filling. Place the veal fillets lengthwise on top of the filling. Finish with the rest of the filling. Smooth the top with a palette knife and bang the tin on the surface again.
6 Brush the overhanging edges of pastry with egg. Lay the rectangular piece of pastry on top, press the two edges together firmly, fold them inwards and crimp them nicely to form a decorative border. Brush with egg, make two steam holes in the top. Make decorative shapes with the pastry trimmings, press them into the pastry and brush with the rest of the egg.
7 Heat the oven to 220ºC/Gas 7. Bake the pâté for 45 minutes. Cover with foil if the pastry is getting brown too soon. Remove from the oven and cool.
8 Dissolve the aspic jelly crystals in the water, bring to a boil, add the port and leave to cool. Pour a little of the liquid jelly through the steam holes into the cooled pâté. Leave to set for a bit before adding more. Keep on adding until the jelly reaches the top and is just visible through the steam holes.
9 For the Cumberland sauce, blanch the orange and lemon zests, drain and refresh them in cold water. Dissolve the sugar and allow it to cook to a light caramel. Moisten with the orange and lemon juice. Add the wine, port and redcurrant jelly and simmer gently until reduced to about 150ml. Season with the mustard, horseradish and cayenne pepper. Stir in the cranberries and bring back to the boil. Cool. Add the zests just before serving with the pâté.

Club Sandwich

Recipe by Rolf von Siebenthal

2 chicken breasts, each about 100g
butter for frying
12 slices brown or white bread
75g cream cheese
6 lettuce leaves, washed
2 tbsp mayonnaise
2 tbsp sour cream
8 slices tomato
8 slices hard-boiled egg
4 slices cucumber
salt and freshly ground pepper

4 nice rashers
smoked streaky bacon,
fried till crisp
4 cherry tomatoes

Tip:
Serve with
potato
crisps.

1 Season the chicken breasts and fry in a little butter. Toast the bread. Season the cheese with salt and pepper and spread the slices with it.

2 Shred the lettuce leaves finely and mix with the mayonnaise and sour cream. Season. Make four triple-decker club sandwiches, starting with a slice of toast, followed by some sliced chicken breast and tomato slices. Continue with more toast slices, followed by sliced chicken and egg and cucumber. Finish with the last toast slices.

3 Cut away all crusts, cut each sandwich in half diagonally. Garnish with the bacon slices and cherry tomatoes.

Sesame Rolls with Coleslaw and Roast Beef

Recipe by Rolf von Siebenthal

4 fresh sesame rolls

Coleslaw:
50g white cabbage, thinly shredded
½ a carrot, grated
2 tbsp mayonnaise
a pinch of sugar
salt and freshly ground pepper

75g butter, creamed
a piece each of red, yellow and green pepper, diced small
½ tbsp tomato purée
cayenne pepper, paprika

12 thin slices roast beef
4 leaves lollo rosso lettuce

1 For the coleslaw, mix together the shredded cabbage and carrot with the mayonnaise and sugar. Season to taste. Chill for a few hours before using.

2 Mix the butter with the pepper pieces and tomato purée and season with salt, pepper, cayenne pepper and paprika.

3 Split the sesame rolls, spread both halves with the pepper butter. Sandwich each one with a lettuce leaf, a quarter of the coleslaw and 3 slices of roast beef.

Bagels with Cream Cheese and Smoked Salmon
Recipe by Rolf von Siebenthal

4 fresh bagels (about 10cm in diameter)
a little finely grated horseradish
125g cream cheese
4 fine lettuce leaves
8 slices smoked salmon
salt and freshly ground pepper

1 Split the bagels. Mix the horseradish into the cream and spread it onto the bagels. Lay a lettuce leaf and 2 slices of smoked salmon on the bottom half of each bagel. Leave a bit of lettuce leaf and smoked salmon visible. Put the tops on.

Baguette with Tuna Provençale
Recipe by Rolf von Siebenthal

125g cream cheese
2 sprigs parsley, chopped
4 basil leaves, chopped
a little fresh marjoram, chopped
salt and freshly ground pepper

4 small baguettes
4 small lettuce leaves
125g tinned tuna, drained and flaked

Marinade:
2 tbsp oil
1 tbsp vinegar
1 shallot, finely chopped
3 sprigs parsley, chopped
a bunch of chives, finely chopped

1 Mix the chopped herbs into the cheese and season to taste. Split the baguettes, spread with the cheese mixture, cover each one with a lettuce leaf. Spread the tuna fish over.
2 Mix together the oil, vinegar, shallot, parsley and chives and spoon it over the tuna fish. Put the tops back on again.

Apricot Tart

Recipe by Rolf von Siebenthal

For a quiche tin 16cm in diameter and
3cm deep

150g sweet shortcrust pastry (see recipe
page 193)

35g butter
2 tbsp brown sugar
1 small egg
2 tbsp ground almonds
2 heaped tablespoons plain white flour
grated zest of ½ a lemon
325g apricots, halved and stoned

1 Roll out the pastry and use it to line
the buttered cake tin. Prick the bottom all over with
a fork.

2 Cream together the butter and sugar,
beat in the egg. Carefully fold in the almonds, flour
and lemon zest. Arrange the apricot halves nicely in
the pastry and pour the mixture over.

3 Heat the oven to 200°C/Gas 6. Bake the
tart for about 35 minutes. Cool before slicing.

Fruity Semolina Puddings
with a Blackberry Sauce

Recipe by Rolf von Siebenthal

325ml milk
50g brown sugar
a pinch of agar-agar
35g semolina
grated zest of ½ a lemon

500g blackberries
150g brown sugar
1 tbsp lemon juice

12 slices kiwi
4 strawberries, stalks intact
12 small pieces melon (skinned)

1 Put the milk, sugar and agar-agar in a
saucepan and bring to a boil, add the semolina and
lemon zest and simmer for 4–5 minutes. Pour hot
into buttered ramekins or moulds and chill for
12 hours.

2 Cook the blackberries with the sugar and
lemon juice, stirring. Push through a sieve to eliminate pips, bring back to a boil and simmer for a few
minutes more. Cool.

3 Pour some sauce onto plates, turn out
the semolina puddings on top and garnish with the
prepared fruit.

Lady-Killer in the Kronenhalle

Ladykiller

2 tbsp gin

1 tbsp Cointreau

1 tbsp apricot brandy

4 tbsp passion fruit or maracuja juice

4 tbsp pineapple juice

6–8 ice cubes

Mix together the ingredients with 3–4 ice cubes in a cocktail shaker or blender, strain and pour into a tall glass. Add 3–4 more ice cubes to the drink in the glass. To garnish: a spiral of orange peel, 2 mint leaves, 1 cocktail cherry. Wrap the cherry in the spiral of orange peel to make a rose, stick in the mint leaf and fix it all together with a toothpick. Serve with the drink.

All drinks were created especially for natural**gourmet** by Peter Roth. Wherever possible, he used organic products like orange juice, white wine or beer.

taking long minutes
to wind down the day

forget the year
look forward to the month

Nectar
1 tbsp white peach liqueur
2 tsp Maracuja liqueur
3 tbsp apricot nectar
5 tbsp well chilled champagne
5–6 ice cubes

and hang on to the moment
with cheers

Mix together all the ingredients except the champagne in a cocktail shaker with the ice cubes and give it a good, brief shake. Strain into a well chilled champagne glass. Fill up with champagne and stir gently.

> **Encounters can lead to relationships – maybe for just an hour, maybe for a whole lifetime.**

Mix together all the ingredients in a cocktail shaker or blender with 3–4 of the ice cubes. Strain and pour into a tall glass filled with 3–4 ice cubes. For the garnish, fix some apple slivers, a mint leaf and a cocktail cherry with a toothpick and perch on the edge of the glass.

Traveller's Punch

2 tbsp dark rum

1 tbsp Maracuja liqueur

1 tsp grenadine syrup

1 tsp lemon juice

125ml pineapple juice

6–8 ice cubes

Jogging

3 tbsp Baileys Irish Cream

100ml milk

1 egg yolk

1 tsp caster sugar

3–4 ice cubes

Mix together all the ingredients in a blender or cocktail shaker. Strain, and pour into a tall glass.

Peter Roth
Head bartender, "Kronen-
halle," Zurich
Born November 15, 1951
World-champion title in mixing drinks with his own creation, the "Lady-Killer"
Countless national and international awards
Author of several cocktail recipe books

For 20 years, Peter Roth has
been the star bartender at the
legendary Kronenhalle Bar,
which is a safe haven for a
host of habitués, artists, writ-
ers, bankers, captains of industry and international personalities. They come in and
drop anchor whenever and as
often as possible – to catch
their breath, for a quick drink
or longer, for an unexpected
encounter with well-known
faces, to see and be seen. As
low-key and unassuming as
the bar – and Peter Roth –
appear at first glance, just as
surprising and fascinating is
the discovery of qualities that
only reveal themselves upon
closer examination. Here, the
passionate devotion to the
job, the consummate profes-
sionalism, the unobtrusive
service and the attention to
detail – there, the tasteful,
high-ceilinged room com-
pletely outfitted in mahogany,
with originals by Picasso,
Miró and Klee casually hung
on the walls, as well as tables and lamps that are origi-
nal works of art by Diego
Giacometti. And all of this is
arranged with such great care
that the people remain the
center of attention – a cause
which Peter Roth champions
with his mind, heart and soul,
every day.

AN ENCOUNTER. The magic of coincidence – an unin-
tentional act of providence with multiple choice, the eternally un-
changing equation with two unknowns and ever-new results, yet everything
is still wide open and nothing is assumed. Jump in or stay out – whichever: It's not possible to leap into the same river twice. And so whoever stays out is in and the other way around. What does it matter? The knot is tied and represents that which just seconds ago was an encounter, and becomes, completely unexpected, that which no one is thinking about:

A RELATIONSHIP.

Sandy Gaff
**150ml well chilled
lager**
**150ml well chilled
ginger ale**

Combine in a beer tankard and stir gently.

> " I was a world champion in mixing drinks. Mixing is one thing. To give the guests a special feeling, to recognise their individuality, that's something else. If there were a world-champion title for that, it would mean more to me. "

Virgin Bull

2 dashes lemon juice
1 dash Worcester sauce
a pinch celery salt
a pinch of pepper
3–4 ice cubes
4 tbsp tomato juice
4 tbsp tinned consommé
optional: a little
Tabasco sauce

Mix together the lemon juice, Worcester sauce, celery salt and pepper in a tumbler. Add the ice cubes and fill up with the tomato juice and consommé. Stir, and add Tabasco if wished. Decorate the glass with some celery leaves if wished.

Put the ice cubes in a tall glass, add all the ingredients
and stir.

Take-Off
1 tbsp gin
1 tbsp Campari
5 tbsp orange juice
3–4 ice cubes

Put the ice cubes in a tall glass. Fill up with the vodka, vermouth, grapefruit juice and Bitter Lemon and stir well. Pour the blue Curaçao on top. Impale a grapefruit segment and a cocktail cherry on a toothpick and fix to the edge of the glass.

Manager Drink

1 tbsp vodka

1 tbsp dry vermouth

100ml grapefruit juice

3 tbsp Bitter Lemon

2 tsp blue Curaçao

3–4 ice cubes

Happy Driver

2 tsp grenadine syrup

2 tsp lemon juice

4 tbsp peach nectar

100ml orange juice

6–8 ice cubes

Tip: For those who have not already drunk, felt or read everything on the subject of "bars": Charles Bukowski, *Western Avenue*

Mix the ingredients together with 3–4 ice cubes in a cocktail shaker or blender. Strain into a tall glass filled with 3–4 ice cubes. Impale an orange slice, a mint leaf and a cherry on a toothpick and fix to the glass edge.

Put all the ingredients in a chilled wine glass and stir.
Fix a lemon slice to the side of the glass.

RESTAURANT KRONENHALLE

Diamond Cocktail

1 tbsp elderflower syrup

**100ml well chilled dry
white wine**

**3 tbsp well chilled lemo-
nade**

Blanc Cassis (Kir)

1 tbsp crème de cassis

**100ml well chilled dry
white wine**

**3 tbsp well chilled soda
water**

Put the cassis in a chilled wine glass,
add the white wine and soda water
and stir.

The Kronenhalle Restaurant

Owned since 1922 by the Zumsteg family, who created a myth out of the simple establishment. In
spite of the luxury, you'll find no trace of snobbery in the "Kronenhalle." "Those who don't belong
here will immediately leave again – it is as if a spirit moves throughout these rooms, about which
again opinions differ…" Many of the most famous artists of this century had a close alliance with
the Zumstegs and their "Kronenhalle" and often spent night after night at the family's table in the
brasserie: Miró, Braque, Chagall, Léger, Alberto Giacometti, Thomas Mann, James Joyce, Stravin-
sky, Richard Strauss, Beuys, Warhol. Also Swiss artists like Cuno Armiet, Max Bill, Dürrenmatt,
Lohse, Tinguely and many more left this legacy to a new generation of young Swiss artists. The
"Kronenhalle" is history and the present all at once – and is unlikely to ever exist in any other form
in the future than it does now.

Kronenhalle Restaurant, Rämistrasse 4, 8001 Zurich • Restaurant telephone +41 1 251 66 69 •
Bar telephone +41 1 251 15 97

Charlie 98

3 tbsp white vermouth

**150ml well chilled
lager**

Put the ver-
mouth in a tall
glass, fill up
with lager and
stir gently.

Roland Jöhri (signature)

Jöhri's "Talvo"
St.Moritz

A champagne climate at 1850 metres above sea level. Icy-cold winter nights follow bright sunny days in fur coats and powder snow. Life pulsates in the midst of this dreamy landscape. Sparkling. Vibrating. Beguiling. Stars in the sky and stars at the tables – the fusion of **dreams and reality.**

The Versatile One

As if a restaurant of this standard were not demanding enough – Roland Jöhri still finds time for other creative pursuits. During the past winter the "Talvo" crew cooked and served a delicious three-course meal every Friday night as part of the legendary evening cooking class on the Rhaetian Railway between Chur and St. Moritz. And then there was the teamwork with the airlines Swissair and Sabena, for whom Jöhri developed First Class menus. Or the gourmet line of prepared foods for regular customers who don't want to have to do without Jöhri delicacies at home. Or his commitment to the St. Moritz Gourmet Festival, among whose founders he was. Or the cooking courses, his magnificent wine degustation menus, or …

Already during his apprenticeship, Roland Jöhri began accumulating old and new menus. Today he has over 40,000 of them in his collection, the oldest of which is from the year 1844. His cookbook library comprises over 2000 volumes (dating back to 1509).

Roland Jöhri, St. Moritz. Born in 1943 in Canton Graubünden, he found his way back to his native mountains after his apprenticeship years and working his way through the great restaurants of Switzerland. Together with his wife Brigitte he runs the "Talvo" in St. Moritz-Champfer, which for years has been honoured with 18 Gault-Millau points and 1 Michelin star. Roland Jöhri has developed his own personal cooking style: traditional and regional recipes, which he integrates into his light, sophisticated cuisine with great creativity and intelligence – without sacrificing the naturalness and simplicity of the dishes. For years, Roland Jöhri has been recognised as one of the best cooks in Switzerland, has won numerous awards at international cooking exhibitions, and has already written two cookbooks as well as coauthoring several others. Among other affiliations, the "Talvo" has earned them the designation Relais Gourmand in the exclusive association "Relais et Chateaux," as well as membership in "Les Grandes Tables de Suisse" and in "Le Soste".

*"He cooks the most exquisite
things with cheerful ease, and she,
Brigitte, with her smile, could keep any
depressed soul from committing suicide.
I speak from experience. (…)
In the Jöhris' 'Talvo,' one can hear
me purring happily; I feel as
contented as a kitten there."*
Wolfram Siebeck, food and wine writer

The Bookworm

It's amazing how matter-of-factly Roland Jöhri opens
his treasure vault – as if it were completely normal
to have books from the 16th century in one's book-
cases. Purposefully, he reaches into a row of thick
parchment covers: "This is a first edition by Scappi
[editor's note: 1540-1570, cooked, among others,
for Pope Pius IV]. There are only a few copies in
the whole world. I have one, and another is owned
by Anton Mosimann." He flashes a mischievous
smile of pride and pleasure, and it seems as if Jöhri
can still get as excited as a kid about his rare posses-
sions. "And look at these drawings here: The monks
copied every knife, every kitchen tool, exactly …"
The former farmhouse living room above the restaurant is jam-packed with cookbooks. Old ones, very
old ones, newer ones, and brand-new ones. Books,
books and more books. And all of them exclusively
about eating and drinking. On the shelves, on the
window sills, on the tables, on the chairs – creative
chaos is all around. And scattered about in between
the books, waiting to be discovered and to delight,
are old kitchen utensils, bronze busts, index card
boxes, awards and keepsake photos. Welcome to
paradise for book-loving gourmets, gastronomic
bibliophiles, cooking fanatics and other maniacs!

Roland Jöhri has no airs about him – in spite of his success, he retains his youthful charm and his warmth. Uncomplicated and fun-loving, he looks forward to every opportunity to break out of the everyday kitchen routine – whether it is for a sumptuous picnic at the lake or an early morning banquet with local hunters.

Cent secrets culinaires
Roland Jöhri

For a 500ml-capacity terrine

4 smoked trout fillets
100ml fish stock
300ml whipping cream
3 leaves gelatine, soaked in cold water until floppy and then squeezed out
a little lemon juice
1 tsp chopped dill
2 spinach beet leaves, blanched
2 beefsteak tomatoes, skinned and quartered
coarse salt and freshly ground pepper

Tip:
A pearl barley salad (see recipe page 157) goes well with this dish. Serve it slightly warm with the terrine.

Smoked Trout Terrine

Terrine von der geräucherten Bachforelle auf Gerstensalat

Jöhri's Talvo Capuns

mit Waldpilzen gefüllte Rehschnitzel und Polenta - Auflauf

Graubündner Alpkäse mit Birnenbrot

Tatschküchlein mit Holunderkompott

1 Skin the trout fillets and put the skins in a pan with the fish stock and half the cream. Boil down to reduce to a third of its volume. Strain, discard the skins. Stir in the prepared gelatine leaves and leave until cool but not quite set. Whip the rest of the cream and fold it into the cooled but not set cream-and-stock mixture. Season the mousse with salt, pepper, lemon juice and dill.

2 Line the terrine with clingfilm and lay one of the beet leaves in the bottom. Pour in a thin layer of fish mousse (about ½cm). Lay some trout fillets and tomato pieces on top. Continue with layers of mousse, fish and tomatoes until all are used up. Cover with the second beet leaf and chill under a light weight.

Pearl Barley Salad

50g pearl barley
75g carrots, kohlrabi and courgettes, cut in batons
1 tbsp chopped parsley

2 tbsp sherry vinegar
4 tbsp sunflower oil
coarse salt and freshly ground pepper, sugar

1 Cook the pearl barley in unsalted water to cover for about 1 hour or until just tender. Drain, reserving some of the cooking water. You should have about 150g cooked pearl barley. Mix this together with the vegetables and parsley. Make a dressing with the vinegar, 2 tablespoons of the reserved cooking water, oil, salt, pepper and a pinch of sugar. Pour it over the barley and vegetables and leave to marinate.

Capuns Talvo-Style

300g quark or *fromage frais*
4 eggs
250g plain white flour
2 shallots, finely chopped
25g air-dried beef, finely diced
25g salsiz or other smoked, dried sausage, finely diced
25g cooked ham, finely diced
salt and freshly ground pepper, nutmeg

16 spinach beet leaves, blanched
50g butter
150ml stock
150ml whipping cream
thyme, marjoram, parsley
1 tbsp whipped cream

1 Mix the quark or *fromage frais* with the eggs. Season with salt, pepper and nutmeg. Mix in the flour to make a smooth, thick batter. Soften the shallots in a little butter with the beef, sausage and ham without allowing the shallots to take colour. Stir into the batter. Trim the beet leaves into rectangles about 4 x 8cm. Put about a teaspoon of filling on each one and roll up into neat parcels.

2 Toss the parcels briefly in hot butter, add the stock and cream and cook for 2–5 minutes until just done. Lift them out with a slotted spoon and keep them warm. Reduce the stock slightly and stir in the whipped cream.

Tip:
Capuns can also be sprinkled with grated cheese and finished in the oven.

8 venison escalopes (roe deer), each about 50g
plain white flour
1 tbsp oil

Wild mushroom stuffing:
50g each ceps and chanterelles, chopped
1 shallot, chopped
15g butter
1 tbsp chopped parsley
a little chopped rosemary
75g game (e.g. venison, wild boar), well trimmed
50g foie gras (goose)
1 egg yolk
4 tbsp whipping cream
salt and freshly ground pepper

1 Beat out the venison escalopes thinly between sheets of clingfilm. Lay them side by side on a baking sheet.

2 Sweat the mushrooms and shallots gently in the butter, season lightly. Add the parsley and rosemary and allow to cool. Cut the game and foie gras in small cubes and put in the freezer briefly until firm but not frozen. Mix the egg yolk and cream together and chill thoroughly. Process everything to a smooth purée in a food processor. Season to taste. Add the mushrooms and check the seasoning.

3 Spread the venison escalopes with the stuffing and fold them over. Press the edges together slightly and fix with toothpicks. Season with salt and pepper and dust in flour. Brown lightly on both sides in hot oil. Drain on paper towels and serve at once.

Venison Slices with Wild Mushroom Stuffing

Polenta Soufflés

For 10–12 ramekins

250ml stock
250ml milk
25g butter
100g coarsely ground polenta flour
2 eggs, separated
salt and freshly ground pepper, nutmeg

Tips:
Any surplus polenta can be left to cool, sliced and fried in hot butter. You can also add raisins or finely chopped prunes to the polenta soufflés.

Tip:
Polenta soufflés go well with the escalopes.

1 Put the stock, milk and butter in a saucepan and bring to a boil. Stir in the polenta flour, bring back to the boil and remove from the heat. Cover and leave beside the stove to steep for 30–40 minutes. Allow to get quite cold. Stir in the egg yolks. Beat the egg whites till stiff and fold them in too. Season the mixture with salt, pepper and nutmeg. Butter the dishes and heat the oven to 180°C/Gas 4.

2 Fill the buttered dishes three-quarters full and put them in a roasting pan with hot water to come halfway up the sides. Bake for about 20 minutes or until set.

Engadine Girdle Cakes with Elderberry Compote

Elderberry compote:

250g elderberries

2–3 tbsp caster sugar, or to taste

½ vanilla pod, split

100ml white wine

125ml milk

1 egg

2 tsp caster sugar

3 tbsp sultanas

50g stale sponge cake, crumbled

a pinch of ground cinnamon

25g butter

1 Wash and drain the elderberries. Strip the berries off the stems and cook them with the sugar, vanilla pod and wine. Remove the vanilla pod. Tip the berries into a sieve held over a bowl to catch the juice. Put a third of the berries in the liquidiser and blend until smooth. Push through a sieve to eliminate pips. Mix the purée with the whole berries and stir in a little of the juice.

2 For the girdle cakes, beat together the milk, egg and sugar. Mix in the sultanas, cake crumbs and cinnamon. Let the batter rest a little. Heat the butter in a small, non-stick frying pan and fry the cakes on both sides till golden brown.

3 Arrange on plates, add the warm elderberry compote and serve at once.

4 veal steaks, each about 125g

oil

15g butter

a sprig each of rosemary and thyme

salt and freshly ground pepper

Farce:

75g well trimmed veal

50g foie gras (duck or goose)

1 egg yolk

5 tbsp whipping cream

3 tbsp chopped parsley

a little chopped rosemary and thyme

1 tbsp Cognac

8 shiitake mushrooms, or 4 cep slices about ½cm thick

a piece of caul, soaked in cold water and squeezed out

Capon à l'Orange

1 oven-ready capon, about 2.5kg
3 tbsp peanut oil
200g mixed onions, celeriac, carrots, cubed
3 tbsp dry white wine (e.g. Riesling)
100ml dark veal stock (see recipe page 192)
100ml orange juice
3 tbsp port
100ml meat glaze
50g butter
2 oranges, peeled *à vif*, segments removed
salt and freshly ground pepper

1 Heat the oven to 200ºC/Gas 6. Season the capon, put in a roasting pan with oil and roast for about 1½ hours. Remove the capon from the oven and keep it warm. Tip away the oil from the roasting pan, add the vegetables, moisten with the wine and stock, add the orange juice and port and simmer gently. Stir in the meat glaze and cook the sauce down to the desired consistency. Strain through a sieve or fine muslin and season.

2 Carve the capon and arrange on a serving dish. Fry the orange slices briefly in the hot butter and lay them over the capon pieces. Serve the sauce separately.

Veal Steak Engadine-Style with a Herby Mushroom Overcoat

1 Season the veal steaks and sear them on both sides in hot oil. Add the butter and the herbs. Let the meat cool.

2 For the *farce*, cut the veal in small pieces and put it briefly in the freezer until firm but not frozen. Mix together the foie gras, egg yolk and cream and chill also. Process all the ingredients together in a food processor to a smooth, shiny mass. Add the chopped herbs and Cognac and season to taste. Chill for half an hour.

3 Remove the stalks from the shiitake mushrooms. Fry the mushrooms gently on both sides in olive oil.

4 Heat the oven to 220ºC/Gas 6. Divide the *farce* between the veal steaks, spreading it on evenly. Arrange some mushrooms on top. Wrap in caul and roast in the hot oven for 5–6 minutes. Remove from the oven and allow to rest a little before serving.

Risotto Soup with Ceps

25g butter
1 tbsp chopped shallots
50g risotto rice (e.g. Vialone, Arborio)
1.25 litres chicken stock
200g fresh ceps
100ml + 6 tbsp whipping cream
1 egg yolk

1 Soften the shallots in half the butter with the rice. Add the stock, season to taste and cook gently for 20 minutes. Add a little more liquid if necessary.

2 Slice the ceps and fry briefly in the rest of the butter. Divide between warmed soup bowls.

3 Stir 100ml cream into the soup, bring to a boil. Put in the liquidiser and blend till smooth. Strain, bring to a boil again. Remove the soup from the heat. Mix together the egg yolk and remaining cream and stir it into the soup – it should not boil again or the yolk will curdle. Check for seasoning, adjusting if necessary.

Pan-fried Sea Bass with Mussels and a Warm Salad of Cucumbers, Sun-dried Tomatoes and Olives

300g mussels
200g cockles
4 small scallops
olive oil
2 shallots, sliced
2 cloves garlic, mashed
2 tomatoes, quartered
100g leek, white part only, finely sliced
a sprig each of thyme, rosemary and flat-leaved parsley
100ml dry white wine (e.g. Chardonnay)
2 sprigs basil, leaves stripped off, finely chopped

Salad:
1 gherkin, finely chopped
¼ cucumber, peeled and cubed
25g sun-dried tomatoes, cubed
1 tbsp diced tomato
75g small, stoned black olives
4 tbsp lemon juice
100ml cold-pressed olive oil
coarse salt and freshly ground pepper

4 fillets of sea bass, skin left on, each about 75g

1 Scrub the shellfish thoroughly and rinse several times. Discard any which are not tightly closed. Heat some olive oil in a large, shallow pan, toss in the shellfish, shallots, garlic, tomatoes, leeks, thyme, rosemary and parsley. Stir briefly, add the wine, cover and cook for 3–4 minutes, stirring and shaking the pan. The shellfish should open. Add the chopped basil and some more olive oil. Remove from the heat and allow to cool a little.

2 Mix together the salad ingredients, season to taste and heat through gently. Shell the mussels, cockles and scallops. Put them in a deep dish and put the salad in the middle.

3 Season the fish fillets, fry in hot oil, skin side first, then the other side briefly. Arrange in the dish and serve at once.

Grilled Scallops with Citrus Noodles

8 scallops
250ml fish stock (see recipe page 192)
juice of 4 limes
3 tbsp whipping cream, beaten till stiff
250g ribbon noodles
25 butter
salt and freshly ground pepper
blanched lime zests to garnish

1 Remove the scallops from their shells, trim and clean them.

2 Simmer the stock and lime juice together gently. Whisk in the whipped cream and season to taste.

3 Cook the noodles in boiling salted water until just tender – 6–8 minutes depending on type. Drop the noodles into the lime sauce and turn them until well coated. Fry the scallops briefly on both sides in hot butter.

4 Wind the noodles into nice portions around a fork and lift onto warmed plates. Arrange the scallops on top, garnish with lime zests and serve at once.

Crème Brûlée with Pear Compote

½ vanilla pod, split
150ml milk
375ml whipping cream
50g caster sugar
5 egg yolks (about 125g)
brown sugar

Pear compote:
4 Williams pears
50g vanilla sugar
125ml white wine
125ml water
juice of ½ a lemon

1 Scrape the seeds out of the vanilla pod and put them in a bowl with the milk, cream, sugar and egg yolks. Mix together gently but thoroughly – it should not get too frothy. Let the mixture rest for 1 hour, strain and pour it into ovenproof ramekins. There should be no froth on the top.

2 Heat the oven to 100ºC/Gas ¼. Put a 4mm-thick sheet of cardboard or folded sheets of newspaper in a saucepan or roasting pan, place the ramekins on top and add water to come a third of the way up the sides. Bake the custards for about 1½ hours, cool and chill them overnight, if possible.

Before serving, heat the grill to maximum, sprinkle the custards with brown sugar and grill till the sugar is nicely caramelised.

3 For the pear compote, put the vanilla sugar, wine, water and lemon juice in a saucepan and bring to a boil. Poach the cleaned, evenly sliced pears in the mixture until tender. Lift out and arrange them in small dessert bowls, pour the juice over. Set a bowl of pears and a soufflé on each large serving plate.

Prune Mousse
with Glühwein Sabayon

For about 6 servings:

75g prunes
300ml Glühwein made with red wine and Glühwein spices
3 egg yolks
2 tbsp caster sugar
1 sheet gelatine, soaked in cold water
1 tbsp coffee liqueur
1 tbsp Cognac
a pinch of ground cinnamon
a pinch of mixed spice
175ml whipping cream

Glühwein Sabayon:
3 egg yolks
250ml Glühwein (from poaching the prunes)
1 sheet gelatine, soaked in cold water and squeezed out

whipped cream, to garnish (optional)

1 Soak the prunes in the Glühwein for 2 days, then simmer them until tender. Remove the stones and chop finely. Reserve the Glühwein.

2 Beat the egg yolks with the sugar. Squeeze out the gelatine and dissolve it in the liqueur and Cognac over gentle heat. Add to the eggs and sugar with the cinnamon and mixed spice. Whip the cream and fold in all but 2 tablespoons, as well as the chopped prunes. Chill the mousse.

3 Shortly before serving, beat the egg yolks in a bain-marie and mix in the Glühwein carefully. Stir in the prepared gelatine and the remaining cream. Pour some sabayon into the middle of each plate and arrange ovals of mousse on top. Garnish, if wished, with swirls of whipped cream.

Upside-down Apple Tartlets
with Sour Cream Ice

For four 8cm-diameter tartlet moulds

Sour Cream Ice:
150g caster sugar
5 tbsp water
650g sour cream
2 tbsp honey
juice of 3 lemons

Apple Tartlets:
4 discs of puff pastry, each about 10cm across
100g marzipan
4 apples (e.g. Boskoop), peeled and sliced
a little lemon juice
100g butter
200g caster sugar
2 tbsp Calvados
5 tbsp whipping cream
butter
caster sugar

1 Make the sour cream ice first: put the sugar and water in a saucepan and bring to a boil. Stir this syrup into the sour cream with the honey and lemon juice. Put in the freezer, remove after 10 minutes and stir thoroughly. Repeat this process several times to ensure even freezing and to prevent formation of ice crystals.

2 Butter the tartlet moulds and sprinkle with sugar. Prick the puff pastry rounds all over with a fork and spread with marzipan. Arrange the apple slices on top, neatly fanned out, and sprinkle

with a little lemon juice. Melt the butter and sugar together in a small pan and cook to a rich caramel. Add the Calvados and the cream and cook down a bit. Pour the caramel into the tartlet moulds and leave to cool. Invert the caramelised moulds over the pastry rounds and immediately slide a palette knife or fish slice underneath and set them right side up again, so that the puff pastry is on top.

3 Heat the oven to 180ºC/Gas 4. Bake the tartlets for 15–20 minutes. Turn them out immediately so that the apples are on top and serve each one with a scoop of sour cream ice.

Sunday morning.

Calm lies over the hills. Last night it finally rained, the air is fresh, and the sound of

church bells wafts clearly up from the lake. The cornfields sway in soft waves as the wind roams gently across the countryside. The peaks of the Alps glow in the light of dawn while silent and sleepy farms and hamlets are lost in daydreams. Somewhere down the lake a few cowbells chime. Fritz will have finished smoking his cigar soon, the stalls are cleaned out and the cows have been herded out to pasture. Sunday morning in the hills. It is still quiet. Soon Martha will spruce up her small rural pub; the weather is good, and the first bicycles are already whirring at high speed along the narrow streets. It's Sunday morning over at the "Schäfli," too. Today and tomorrow there will be no big cars parked in front of the little country restaurant; Wolfgang will not stand at the stove in his grey pin-striped trousers and white cook's jacket; he won't – with his left hand resting on his back – duck his angular head slightly when he steps through the low door leading from his realm into the restaurant to greet his guests. Today and tomorrow, no glasses will sparkle on the tables, and no medley of voices will fill the cosy dining rooms; Josef will not go down into the wine cellar and take a Château Margaux 1983 carefully from the shelf; Simi will not be meticulously garnishing appetizers in the kitchen today and tomorrow; and Marlis, the proprietress, will not be making sure, with a wink of the eye and a keen sense of her surroundings, that everything goes at it should. Today and tomorrow, the "Schäfli" is closed. Nothing will hint at the fact that a little culinary oasis is hiding in the inconspicuous half-timbered house – and that a wolf is lurking inside the sheep's hide.

Wolfgang Kuchler's "Taverne zum Schäfli"

The wolf in sheep's clothing.
Or why Wolfgang Kuchler is so immodestly modest.

The sheep's hide – that's the little half-timbered house, the cosy and simple country restaurant with a few tables, serving simple and hearty dishes like mashed potatoes, saddle of veal or sauerkraut soup. It's an unobtrusive wine cellar with mountains of bottles and wooden crates. It's a highly qualified team of four people – two in the kitchen and two in service – and their unpretentious warmth. As for the wolf, you only get a glimpse of him upon closer inspection.

Wolfgang Kuchler is unbridled and extravagant in his pursuit of quality. He braises the saddle of veal in the most magnificent wine, such as most would hardly dare to drink. He is obsessed by the best, whatever that might be – his suppliers suffer and rejoice with him. And in his wine cellars are stored the best wines in the world, an "open sesame" for wine aficionados.

Independence is an existentially important feeling in life for Wolfgang Kuchler – to be beholden to nothing and no one and to have the freedom to act as he sees fit at every moment.

Wolfgang Kuchler is not at all modest. He is excessive in his demands on himself and others. That's why he needs a realm that he can model exactly according to his own ideas.

Wolfgang Kuchler is modest. His modesty is a testament to his individuality – and to his own, very personal world. This is all he needs and wants.

2 courgettes, sliced

4 lobsters, cooked and shelled

150g mixed vegetables (carrots, leeks, celeriac), finely diced, blanched

50g potatoes, finely diced, fried

100ml olive oil vinaigrette (see recipe page 191)

1 tbsp each chopped chives and parsley

herbs to garnish

Wolfgang Kuchler, Wigoltingen
Born in 1950 in Stuttgart, Germany, he is one of the
most individualistic chefs in Switzerland. His small, cosy
restaurant in the rural seclusion of Thurgau is today one
of the favourite places for gourmets to gather. His cuisine, fine rather than fancy, distinguishes itself through
simplicity and the highest standards of quality and preparation. Together with his wife Marlis and two other
colleagues, he manages to combine culinary skill with
sincerity. His wine cellar is one of the largest and best
in Switzerland. In the past, Wolfgang Kuchler has parti-
cipated in numerous culinary arts exhibitions and gained
professional experience both at home and abroad.

Kuchler's Menu

Warm Lobster Salad à la "Schäfli"

∞

Red Mullet Fillets in a
Light Garlic Sauce

∞

Boned Best Ends of Neck of Lamb
with onion gratin
with Basil and Parmesan
Maxim's Potatoes.

∞

Chocolate Soufflés
with
Three Sorts of Oranges

Warm Lobster Salad à la "Schäfli"

1 Blanch the courgette slices and drain.
Arrange them in circles on flat plates. Cut each lobster in 8–10 pieces and place on top of the courgette
slices. Heat the vegetables and potatoes in the vinaigrette, add the chives and parsley and pour this over
the lobster. Garnish with more herbs and serve at
once.

Red Mullet Fillets in a Light Garlic Sauce

Tip:
Fillets of
monkfish or
sole can
be used
instead of
red mullet,
if wished.

2 cloves garlic, halved, green shoots removed
2 shallots, finely chopped
500g fillets of red mullet
2 tomatoes, skinned, seeded and diced
1 bunch of spring onions, trimmed but green part left on
a little butter
1 bunch chives, finely chopped
100ml dry white Bordeaux
seasonal vegetables to garnish (e.g. leeks, artichokes, carrots)
50g butter, chilled
salt and freshly ground pepper

1 Heat the oven to 200°C/Gas 6. Put the garlic and shallots in a lightly buttered and seasoned ovenproof dish and lay the fish fillets on top. Sprinkle the tomato cubes, spring onions and chives over the fish, season and scatter butter dots on top. Pour the wine over and bake for about 5 minutes until just cooked, basting once with the wine.

2 Prepare a garnish with the seasonal vegetables. Place the fish fillets on top. Boil down the fish cooking liquid until somewhat reduced and whisk in the chilled butter. Pour it over the fish and serve at once.

Rack of Lamb with an Artichoke and Tomato Crust

2 best ends of neck of lamb, well trimmed
(each about 200g, after boning and
trimming)
1 tbsp olive oil
1 tbsp Dijon mustard
2 cooked artichoke hearts, cubed
2 tomatoes, skinned, seeded and cubed
25g butter
2 tbsp mixed chopped herbs (parsley,
tarragon, basil)
75g fresh white breadcrumbs
salt and freshly ground pepper

1 Heat the oven to 200°C/Gas 6. Season
the lamb and sear it in hot olive oil in a frying pan
on the skin side. Bake for 8–10 minutes, remove
from the oven (but leave the oven on) and spread
with the mustard. Leave in a warm place.

2 Heat half the butter in a small frying pan
and fry the artichokes with the tomatoes. Add the
herbs. In a separate pan fry the breadcrumbs in the
rest of the butter and mix with the artichokes and
tomatoes. Press this mixture firmly into the lamb.
Finish the lamb in the oven, if possible using good
top heat so that the crust browns nicely.

3 Serve with an onion gratin and Maxim's
Potatoes.

Onion Gratin with Basil and Parmesan

300g onions, sliced
2 cloves garlic, mashed
a knob of butter
1 tbsp olive oil
100ml white wine
2 tbsp snipped basil leaves
3 tbsp whipping cream
2 tbsp Parmesan, finely grated
salt and freshly ground pepper

1 Soften the onions and garlic in the butter
and oil without allowing them to brown. Moisten
with the wine, cover and cook over moderate heat
until tender. Season and add the basil leaves. Tip
into a buttered ovenproof dish, spoon the cream
over and sprinkle with Parmesan.

2 Heat the oven to 240°C/Gas 9, preferably with good top heat. Bake for about 10 minutes.

Maxim's Potatoes

300g potatoes, peeled and thinly sliced
75g butter, melted and cooled
salt

1 Heat the oven to 200°C/Gas 6, preferably with good top heat. Arrange the potatoes in
closely overlapping slices in a buttered ovenproof
dish. Pour over the butter and bake for 12–15
minutes. Press them together a bit and serve at
once.

1 Cut away the peel and pith from both sorts of oranges with a sharp knife, right down to the flesh. Cut out the segments of flesh from between the membranes. Squeeze out the membranes and reserve the juice. (You should have about 3 tablespoons.) Cook the kumquats gently together with the sugar, reserved orange juice and Grand Marnier till syrupy.

2 Heat the oven to 180°C/Gas 4. Butter the soufflé dishes and sprinkle them with sugar. Beat the egg yolks with the butter and sugar until creamy. Fold in the Grand Marnier and the melted chocolate. Beat the egg whites with a tablespoon of sugar until stiff but still creamy. Fold them carefully into the chocolate mixture. Fill the dishes three-quarters full with the mixture and place in a roasting pan with water to come halfway up the sides of the dishes. Bake in the lower part of the oven for 12–15 minutes or until just set and nicely risen.

3 Divide the orange slices and kumquats between the plates, run a knife around the edge of the dishes and turn the soufflés out on top of the fruit. Serve at once.

Chocolate Soufflés with Three Sorts of Oranges

For 4 ramekins

2 blood oranges
2 oranges
8 kumquats
1 tbsp caster sugar
3 tbsp orange juice
3 tbsp Grand Marnier

Soufflés:
2 eggs, separated
50g soft butter
25g caster sugar + 1 tbsp
1 tbsp Grand Marnier
50g bitter chocolate, melted
butter and sugar for the dishes

Lemongrass Soup with Curry and Leeks

100g leeks, carrots and celeriac, diced small
5 stems lemongrass, finely sliced
2 tbsp extra-virgin olive oil
1 clove garlic, mashed with a little salt
a walnut-sized piece fresh ginger, grated
turmeric
1 tbsp curry powder
1 litre light chicken stock
200ml unsweetened coconut milk
1 leek, sliced
salt and white pepper

1 Soften the leeks, carrots, celeriac and lemongrass in the oil without allowing them to brown. Remove from the heat, stir in the garlic, ginger and spices. Moisten with the stock, cover the pan and cook over very gentle heat for 1–2 hours. Add a little more stock if necessary. Stir in the coconut milk, bring briefly to a boil. Blend till smooth in the liquidiser and push through a sieve, pressing down hard to extract all the flavour from the fibrous, woody lemongrass stems.

2 Blanch the sliced leeks. Bring the soup back to a boil, whisk together again and garnish with the leek slices.

Tip:
To raise the tone a bit, you can add some grilled scallops or langoustines to the soup.

Soup of Puy Lentils with a Splash of Balsamic Vinegar

2 rashers smoked streaky bacon, cut in strips
2 tbsp extra-virgin olive oil
100g mixed vegetables (celery, carrots, spring onions), finely sliced
2 sun-dried tomatoes, diced
50g shallots, finely chopped
1 tbsp tomato purée
2 tomatoes, roughly chopped
1 bouquet garni
several parsley stalks
50g Puy lentils
1 tsp Meaux mustard seeds
3 tbsp each Madeira, red wine and orange juice
500ml light veal stock (see recipe page 192)
100ml whipping cream
Balsamic vinegar
salt and freshly ground pepper

1 Fry the bacon strips in the oil until crispy. Add the vegetables, sun-dried tomatoes and shallots to the pan and allow them to soften a little. Throw in the tomato purée, fresh tomatoes, shallots, bouquet garni and parsley stalks and cook them all together briefly. Add the lentils and mustard seeds, stir briefly and moisten with the Madeira, wine and orange juice. Pour in the stock and simmer gently for about 1 hour. Finally, stir in the cream and season with Balsamic vinegar, salt and pepper. Remove the bouquet garni. Blend until smooth in a liquidiser and push through a sieve. Serve sprinkled with a little olive oil.

Tuna Carpaccio with Wasabi Vinaigrette

4 tbsp mixed diced vegetables (carrots, celeriac, leeks)
1 large potato
200g fresh tuna, cut from the centre
sea salt and freshly ground pepper

Wasabi Vinaigrette:
250ml best quality olive oil
3 tbsp Champagne vinegar
1 tbsp Balsamic vinegar
3 tbsp lemon juice
1 tbsp soy sauce
25g wasabi paste (green horseradish mustard)
salt and freshly ground pepper

1 Blanch the vegetables briefly. Peel the potato and cut in tiny dice. You should have about 2 tablespoons. Blanch, drain and fry until golden and crusty.

2 Slice the tuna not too thinly, arrange overlapping slices in a circle on chilled plates. Season and sprinkle with the diced vegetables and potatoes. Mix all the ingredients together for the wasabi vinaigrette and drizzle it over the tuna shortly before serving.

Braised Calves' Cheeks in a Merlot Sauce with Vegetable Chartreuses

For 4 bottomless rings, each about 7–9cm in diameter

Calves' Cheeks:
4 calves' cheeks, trimmed of fat, gristle and skin
a little flour
25g butter
2 tbsp olive oil
500g onions, leeks, celeriac and carrots, finely diced
1 tbsp tomato purée
¾ litre red wine
1 litre dark veal stock (see recipe page 192)

a bouquet garni
salt and freshly ground pepper

Chartreuses:
200g French beans
100g carrots
100g kohlrabi
25g soft butter
200g rosemary-flavoured mashed potatoes (see recipe page 176)

1 Season the calves' cheeks, sprinkle with flour and brown on all sides in a casserole in the hot butter and oil. Remove. In the same casserole, fry the vegetables and tomato purée slowly, moisten with the wine and simmer for a minute or two. Add the stock, replace the calves' cheeks in the casserole, add the bouquet garni and bake in a 200ºC/Gas 6 oven for 2 hours.

2 Cut the beans, carrots and kohlrabi in strips the same height as the rings. Blanch them separately. Butter the rings and set them on a baking sheet or tray lined with greaseproof paper. Line the rings with the blanched vegetables, standing them up (alternating colours) all around the inside. Cover with clingfilm and set on one side. Make the rosemary-flavoured mashed potatoes.

3 Lift the calves' cheeks out of the cooking liquid. Strain the sauce and degrease it with paper towels. Check the seasoning. Heat the vegetable chartreuses briefly in the oven, set them on warm plates and fill with the mashed potatoes. Slide the greaseproof paper carefully out from underneath and lift off the rings. Arrange the meat attractively next to the chartreuses and spoon the sauce over.

To skim off surplus fat from sauces, stocks or soups (**'degreasing'**, in kitchen parlance), lay several changes of paper towels on the top of the liquid. The paper will absorb the fat which can then be discarded. Alternatively, let the liquid stand overnight in a cool place and lift or spoon off the congealed or hardened fat.

Sautéd Langoustines with Rosemary-Flavoured Mashed Potatoes

1 sprig rosemary, roughly chopped
50g clarified butter or a mixture of butter and oil
500g potatoes, peeled
a pinch of saffron powder
100ml milk
100ml whipping cream
2 tbsp extra-virgin olive oil
nutmeg
sea salt

8 raw langoustines, halved and shelled
1 tbsp olive oil
15g butter
1 tbsp flat-leaved parsley, chopped
2 tbsp olive oil vinaigrette (see recipe page 191)
salt and freshly ground pepper

1 First make the mashed potatoes: stew the rosemary gently in the butter for an hour, strain and cool. Cook the potatoes in boiling salted water with the saffron until soft, drain and mash them and add the remaining ingredients. Spread out a good dollop of mash in the middle of each plate.

2 Season the langoustines and sear for 30 seconds in the hot oil and butter. Stir in the parsley. Arrange on top of the mashed potatoes and drizzle the vinaigrette over.

Fillet of Veal with Caramel Sauce

400g fillet of veal, trimmed and tied
1 tbsp mixed grapeseed oil and melted butter
salt and freshly ground pepper
4 heads of chicory (Belgian endive)
100g mixed onions, leeks and celeriac
1 tbsp olive oil
100ml light veal stock (see recipe page 192)
juice of ½ a lemon

Sauce:
50g caster sugar
200ml carrot juice, freshly pressed
Balsamic vinegar
50g chilled butter

1 Heat the oven to 200ºC/Gas 6. Season the veal and roast for 8–10 minutes in the oil and butter until just cooked but still nicely pink inside. Leave to rest in a warm place.

2 Trim and wash the chicory but leave it whole. Slice the onions, leeks and celeriac and sweat briefly in the olive oil. Lay the chicory on top, add the stock and lemon juice and season to taste. Cover the pan and cook gently until tender. (Test with a fork.)

3 For the sauce, dissolve the sugar and cook until caramelised to a rich dark brown. Add the carrot juice and Balsamic vinegar, bring to a boil and cook down hard to reduce to about 100ml. Whisk in the butter bit by bit.

4 Serve the braised chicory with the sliced veal over the sauce.

Duck Sausages with Puy Lentils

250g skinless, boneless duck leg meat, well trimmed

50g calf's sweetbreads, soaked and trimmed

50g duck foie gras

100g white bread, crusts removed

1 egg

100–150ml whipping cream

2 tbsp tinned truffle juice, optional

a little Cognac or Armagnac

salt and freshly ground pepper

a piece of pig's caul, soaked in white wine

Lentils:

100g Puy lentils, soaked overnight in cold water

olive oil

25g rindless streaky bacon, cut in strips

50g mixed vegetables (carrots, leeks, celeriac), cubed

1 tbsp tomato purée

1 gherkin

a few capers

2 tbsp finely chopped flat-leaved parsley

a few strips of orange and lemon peel

a splash of Balsamic vinegar

3 tbsp port

100ml chicken stock

a little chilled butter

butter for frying the sausages

1 Put the duck flesh, sweetbreads and foie gras through a mincer, or process finely in a food processor together with the remaining ingredients. Beat over ice until smooth, season well. Make little 'sausages' each weighing about 30g and wrap them in pieces of caul.

2 Blanch the lentils and drain them. Fry the bacon gently in the oil until the fat runs, add the vegetables and cook until just soft. Add the lentils, and all the remaining ingredients (except the chilled butter), and cook for 8–12 minutes until the lentils are tender. Whisk in the chilled butter at the end.

3 Fry the sausages gently in a little butter. Divide the lentils between the plates and serve the sausages on top.

d Chicory

Mutter Margarete's Apple Crumble

For a large baking tray about 30x40cm, serving about 12 people

Yeast pastry:
250g plain white flour
15g yeast
100ml milk
2 tbsp caster sugar
a pinch of salt
75g butter
1 egg
grated lemon zest

Crumble:
400g plain white flour
400g butter, cut in pieces

350g caster sugar
1 vanilla pod, split, seeds scraped out
a pinch of salt

1½–2kg apples (Boskoop or other cooking apple)
2 tbsp sultanas, soaked in rum
2 tbsp caster sugar
2 tbsp ground almonds
1 tsp cinnamon
a few slivered hazelnuts
butter dots for the top

1 For the pastry, put the flour in a bowl and make a well in the centre. Crumble in the yeast and mix in a little milk and the sugar. Sprinkle some flour on top and leave to sponge for 15 minutes. Add the rest of the milk and the remaining ingredients, mix well and knead thoroughly. Cover and leave in a warm place until doubled in bulk.

2 For the crumble, mix together the flour, butter, sugar, vanilla seeds and salt, rubbing between the palms of your hands until nice and crumbly.

3 Butter the baking sheet and heat the oven to 180ºC/Gas 4. Roll out the pastry thinly and put it on the baking sheet, prick with a fork all over. Peel the apples and arrange them over the pastry. Scatter the soaked sultanas over. Mix together the sugar, ground almonds and cinnamon and sprinkle these all over the pastry. Cover with the crumble. Scatter the hazelnuts and butter dots on top and bake the crumble for 35–40 minutes.

Vanilla Ice Cream with a Splash of Balsamic Vinegar

10 egg yolks
200g caster sugar
a pinch of salt
800ml milk
2 vanilla pods
300ml double cream
a few drops of aged Balsamic vinegar

1 Beat together the egg yolks, sugar and salt until creamy. Split the vanilla pods and scrape out the seeds and soft insides. Put these and the pods in a saucepan with the milk and bring to a boil. Add to the egg yolk mixture and return everything to the pan. Reheat, stirring constantly, until just below boiling. The cream should lightly coat the back of a spoon. Remove from the heat, strain, remove the pods and stir the custard over cold water to prevent further cooking. Add the cream and freeze the mixture.

2 Scoop out some ice cream and serve on well chilled plates. Sprinkle with a little Balsamic vinegar.

Tip: According to my mother (the Margarete in the recipe title), the crumble is best served warm.

„Everything simple is beautiful,
everything beautiful is simple."

Anton Mosimann, London. Born in 1947 in Switzerland, where he also grew up, Anton Mosimann has lived in Great Britain for many years. Already in his younger years, Anton Mosimann was the head chef at London's renowned Dorchester Hotel and was awarded two Michelin stars. Today, Mosimann is one of the most well-known cooks in the world. In 1988, he founded his own exclusive dining club, "Mosimann's," in an old church. Memberships for it are highly sought after. Club members include royalty, politicians, business tycoons and famous personalities from around the world. In 1996, Anton Mosimann opened his own cooking academy in London. Here, both professional and hobby cooks meet regularly for workshops and seminars. Mosimann's library, which contains one of the largest private cookbook collections in the world, is located in the academy. Anton Mosimann is the author of several cookbooks and hosts televised cooking shows in England and Switzerland.

Cuisine Naturelle. In 1985, with his "cuisine naturelle," Anton Mosimann initiated a new cooking philosophy in England – light and natural, without fats and alcohol. A British commentator remarked later that England's culinary history can be divided into exactly two periods: the before-Mosimann era and the since-Mosimann era.

The most important milestones in my life were ...

... my decision, after completing my cook's apprenticeship, to vie for a job in one of the best hotel kitchens in Switzerland, at the Palace Hotel in Villars. I was 17 years old at the time and knew that I only wanted to learn from the best teachers. Another important experience for me was when, five years later, I got the chance as head chef to run the restaurant in the Swiss Pavilion at Expo 1970 in Japan. And five years later, I became head chef at the legendary Dorchester Hotel in London. I was 28 years old and the youngest chef to ever hold such a position.

What's Swiss about me is ...

... my quest for perfection. I appreciate punctuality. I am adaptable – I think this is a very Swiss trait and has been a basis for my success.

Life in England ...

... is my kind of life. I am happy here. I like the English art of understatement, the open-minded, generous lifestyle, the respect for rules and rituals. I never fail to be impressed by the way style and manners are cultivated: it may be 30°C in the shade, but an English gentleman would never, under any circumstances, take off his jacket. Or the horse races in Ascot, the polo matches, the royal family, the outstanding schools with their strict regulations – that for me is as much a part of English life as the Matterhorn is a part of Switzerland.

For me, holidays mean ...

... nothing. I never take a holiday. Why should I? My work is like a holiday for me. I look forward every day to what is ahead. Every day brings a surprise – life is exciting, and life is happening NOW. Yesterday is past, and tomorrow is not yet here. Right now is the only thing that counts. So I make the best of it.

The key to success?

I don't know what the key is. I only know that I could not have achieved what I have without enthusiasm and a positive attitude towards life. Certainly my creativity as a cook is part of it, too. Creativity is a gift, and I am very thankful for it. Important to success, in whatever area it is, is the will to be better, to win. For me, "winning" is a key word. It has been ever since I was a young wrestler and 100-metre runner, and it still means a lot to me today.

One of the most beautiful moments for me was ...

... a few years ago, when I received an Honorary Doctorate of Culinary Arts from Johnson & Wales University in Charleston/U.S.A. Another highlight was a state banquet in Prague Castle that was organised by Prince Charles and Czech President Václav Havel. Sir Georg Solti conducted the Prague Philharmonic there, Kiri Te Kanawa sang, and Mosimann cooked. Doesn't that sound grand?

The most unconventional meal ...

... was the one I cooked for the homeless in London. I was very moved.

Pet peeves, crazy habits or passions?

My goodness. I'm crazy about music. Whether I'm working at my desk or rummaging around in my library, whether I am at the club or at the cooking academy, I need music turned up full volume. Another passion is cars – my Jaguars and old-timers.

Dreams and wishes?

I am a dreamer. And many of my dreams have come true. My next goal is to build a museum which, among other things, will house my library of over 4000 cookbooks, which date back to the 14th century.

If my wife were to describe me, she would say I am ...

... a workaholic. And it's true. I work seven days a week, and there isn't a day that that bothers me. She would probably also say that I enjoy all beautiful things, and always make the best of every situation.

The last word ...

... You never get a second chance to make a first impression.

Scottish Salmon and Halibut Sashimi with Spring Onion, Toasted Sesame and Coriander

Sashimi dressing:
2 tbsp sake
3 tbsp mirin
a piece of kelp (kombu), 1 x 2.5cm, wiped
1 tbsp tamari sauce
225ml dark soy sauce
1 tsp bonito flakes

250g fresh salmon, finely sliced
200g fresh halibut, finely sliced
2 tbsp finely sliced spring onions
2 tsp sesame seeds, toasted
12 coriander leaves
salt and freshly ground pepper

1 Make the dressing ahead: heat together the sake and mirin, then light them with a match to burn off the alcohol. Add all the remaining ingredients, bring to the boil and simmer gently for 5 minutes. Remove from the heat and leave to stand in a cool place for at least 5–6 hours.

2 Spoon about 2 teaspoons dressing onto each plate and season lightly with salt and pepper. Arrange the halibut and the salmon attractively on the plates. Ensure that the fish is evenly distributed between the plates, then brush generously with more dressing. Sprinkle the spring onions and sesame seeds on top and garnish with the coriander leaves.

Caesar Salad

2 heads cos lettuce

Caesar dressing:
1 egg yolk
1 tsp Dijon mustard
1 tsp sherry vinegar
½ tsp Balsamic vinegar
2 tbsp vegetable oil
150ml cold-pressed olive oil
4 tbsp chicken stock
3 tbsp grated Parmesan
2 anchovy fillets, mashed
salt and freshly ground pepper

Croutons:
2 tbsp olive oil
25g butter
1 small clove garlic, mashed
2 pieces white sliced bread, cut in cubes
50g freshly grated Parmesan
finely chopped chives

1 Trim the lettuce, discarding the outer leaves and separating the inner leaves. Wash and spin in a salad spinner.

2 For the dressing, beat together the egg yolk, mustard and vinegars using a hand-held blender or mixer. Beat in the oil and stock by turns. Finally, add the Parmesan and anchovy fillets and season to taste.

3 Heat together the oil and butter and soften the garlic gently in them. Remove the garlic, add the bread cubes and fry till golden brown over moderate heat. Drain on paper towels and put them back in the wiped out pan. Sprinkle a third of the grated cheese over the croutons, and reheat briefly.

4 Pour a tablespoon of dressing on each plate, arrange 3 or 4 lettuce leaves on top, drizzle with more dressing and sprinkle with more Parmesan. Continue with more lettuce leaves, dressing and cheese. Finish with chives and the warm cheese croutons.

1 Hold the tomatoes upright, stem uppermost. Cut a thick slice from each of the four sides so as to leave a square core in the middle. Discard the core. Flatten the slices gently with the palm of your hand and trim into neat rectangles. Cut the Mozzarella into slices about the same size as the tomatoes and trim them to fit. Wash the basil and strip off the leaves.

2 Line the terrine generously with clingfilm. Arrange a neat layer of tomatoes, rounded side downwards, to fit snugly in the bottom of the terrine. Season well and cover with a layer of Mozzarella slices and some basil leaves. Continue in this way with the remaining ingredients, seasoning as you go and finishing with a layer of tomatoes. Bring the clingfilm up over the tomatoes to enclose completely. Cut a piece of cardboard to fit the top of the terrine, lay it on the terrine and put a light weight on top. Chill for several hours.

3 Turn the terrine carefully out, remove the clingfilm and cut in thick slices. Arrange on plates, sprinkle with oil and vinegar and garnish with a basil leaf.

Tomato, Mozzarella and Basil Terrine

For a small, deep terrine 20cm long

12–14 large, ripe plum tomatoes
(San Marzano)
500g Mozzarella
a large bunch of basil
salt and freshly ground pepper
4 sprigs of basil
extra-virgin olive oil
Balsamic vinegar

Beef Tournedos with Sweet Peppers and Black Bean Sauce

4 tournedos, cut from a fillet of beef, each about 150g

1 medium red, yellow and green pepper

200ml dark veal stock (see recipe, page 192)

4 tsp fermented black beans

2 small garlic cloves, peeled

a 2½ cm piece fresh ginger, peeled and roughly chopped

1 tbsp olive oil

3 tbsp red wine

2 tbsp fresh coriander leaves

salt and freshly ground pepper

1 Trim the tournedos well. Roast the peppers in a hot oven or grill or sear them over a gas flame. Rub off the skin under running water, remove the cores, seeds and ribs and cut into even strips. Boil down the veal stock until reduced by half.

2 Rinse the black beans under cold water and squeeze dry. Put half into a mortar and grind to a paste with the garlic and ginger.

3 Season the tournedos and fry them in hot oil for 2–3 minutes on each side. Remove from the pan and keep warm. In the same pan, fry the pepper strips quickly. Season and keep warm. Remove any excess oil from the pan, deglaze with the wine, then add the reduced veal stock and black bean paste. Stir together for a few minutes, then add the remaining whole black beans. Coat the tournedos with the sauce and top with the pepper strips. Garnish with the coriander and serve at once.

Whitefish Fillets Oriental-Style

Tip:
Serve the
chicken on
banana
leaves with
coconut rice,
if wished.

4 boneless whitefish fillets (each about 150g), scaled but not skinned

2 tsp sesame oil

3 tbsp each red and yellow peppers cut in ½ cm dice

a walnut-sized piece of ginger, finely sliced

4 spring onions, finely sliced

2 tsp light soy sauce

2 tsp chilli sauce

1 tbsp finely chopped chives

1 tbsp finely chopped fresh coriander

4 tbsp sesame oil

salt and freshly ground pepper

1 Make three neat diagonal slashes in the skin side of the fish fillets, 3mm deep.

2 Oil a grilling tray and heat the grill. Carefully season the fish fillets on both sides and lay them in it. Grill the fish on both sides till lightly golden (approximately 5 minutes). Be careful not to let the fillets dry out – brush with a little more oil if necessary.

3 Put the peppers, ginger and spring onions in a saucepan, add the soy sauce, chilli sauce and herbs and season with salt and pepper.

4 Just before serving, bring the oil to smoking point in a small pan (take great care that the oil does not splash) and add it to the vegetable and soy mixture. Spoon this sauce over the fish while still hot.

Barbecued Honey-Glazed Chicken Breast

Marinade:

100ml light soy sauce

1 tbsp dry mustard powder

1 tbsp clear honey

a 5 cm piece fresh ginger, peeled and grated

1 medium onion, peeled and grated

2 cloves garlic, mashed

1 star anise, crushed

4 maize-fed chicken breasts, each about 150g

salt and freshly ground pepper

1 Mix together the soy sauce and the mustard powder in a china or glass container. Add all the rest of the marinade ingredients and leave to stand for at least 8 hours or overnight.

2 Coat the chicken breasts with the marinade and leave for at least an hour, turning and basting occasionally.

3 Heat a grill or barbecue in good time. Scrape the marinade off the chicken and reserve. Season the chicken and grill for 5–6 minutes on each side, basting occasionally with the reserved marinade.

Cappucino Crème Brûlée

200ml double cream
10g instant coffee granules
½ vanilla pod, split
3 egg yolks
50g caster sugar

Sabayon:
6 egg yolks
75g caster sugar
75ml water
125ml Kahlua

25g brown sugar
ground cinnamon

1 Bring the cream to a boil with the coffee granules and vanilla pod. Whisk together the yolks and sugar and add the hot cream, whisking continuously until thoroughly mixed. Pour the mixture into a clean saucepan. Reheat, stirring continuously, until it thickens and coats the back of a spoon. Remove from the heat immediately and strain. Pour into four coffee cups, and place in the refrigerator to set.

2 For the sabayon, dissolve the sugar in the water and boil to a syrup. Cool. Put the egg yolks, sugar, syrup and Kahlua in a mixing bowl over a pan of simmering water. Do not allow the bottom of the bowl to touch the water. Whisk until thick and creamy.

3 Sprinkle the brown sugar over the chilled crème brûlée and caramelise using a blow-torch.

4 Spoon the sabayon over the cappucino crème and dust with cinnamon.

Bread and Butter Pudding

25g butter
3 small bread rolls
250ml milk
250ml double cream
a pinch of salt
1 vanilla pod, split
3 eggs
125g caster sugar
1 tbsp sultanas, soaked in water
1 tbsp apricot jam, sieved
icing sugar

1 Lightly butter a large ovenproof dish. Slice the rolls and spread with the rest of the butter. Arrange them in the dish. Bring the milk and cream gently to a boil with the salt and vanilla pod.

2 Beat the eggs with the sugar until pale and mousse-like. Add the milk and cream mixture to the eggs, stirring well to mix. Strain into a clean bowl.

3 Drain the sultanas and add them to the bread in the dish along with the milk mixture. The bread will float to the top. Heat the oven to 160ºC/Gas 3.

4 Put some sheets of folded newspaper in a roasting pan and place the prepared dish on top. Add enough hot water to come halfway up the sides of the dish. Bake for 45–50 minutes. The pudding should wobble very slightly in the middle. Remove from the oven and cool a little.

5 Dilute the apricot jam with a little water if necessary and heat it gently. Lightly brush a thin coat of the warm glaze over the top of the pudding. Dust with icing sugar and serve slightly warm.

Apple and Blackberry Crumble

1 Peel and core the apples and cut each one in six pieces. Slice fairly thickly. Melt the butter and fry the apple slices gently. Add the sugar and cinnamon and cook, stirring, until the apples are just done. A little more sugar or cinnamon can be added to taste. Add the blackberries and stir carefully.

2 To make the crumble, cut the butter in dice and rub it into the flour and sugar until crumbly.

3 Heat the oven to 200ºC/Gas 6. Butter some ovenproof soup bowls and spoon in the apples and blackberries. Sprinkle with the crumble and bake until golden brown. Serve with a little cream and raspberry coulis drizzled over the top. Sprinkle with icing sugar and garnish with mint leaves.

Tip:
Pears can be used instead of apples if preferred.

3 large cooking apples (about 900g)
25g butter
150g caster sugar
a pinch of cinnamon (or to taste)
75g fresh blackberries

Crumble:
50g butter, chilled
100g plain white flour
50g caster sugar
mint leaves and icing sugar to garnish

Swiss Plaited Milk Loaf

500g strong white bread flour
25g fresh yeast
200ml milk
1–2 tbsp caster sugar
100g soft butter
1 egg
1 tsp salt
2 tbsp whipping cream

½ an egg, to glaze

1 Put the flour in a mixing bowl, make a well in the centre. Crumble the yeast into the well and add some of the milk and the sugar. Sprinkle a little flour on top and allow to sponge for 15 minutes.

2 Add the remaining ingredients and mix well with a wooden spoon, then knead by hand until the dough starts to come away from the sides of the bowl. Turn out the dough and knead thoroughly, lifting and turning it, until very smooth and elastic. Put the dough back in the bowl, cover with a damp tea-towel and leave to rise in a warm place until doubled in bulk. Knock back the dough and knead it again a little, cut in half and roll out each piece to a long sausage with pointed ends. Plait the two pieces together. Put on a lightly buttered baking sheet, cover with foil and allow to rise again.

3 Heat the oven to 220ºC/Gas 7. Put a roasting pan of water in the bottom of the oven. Glaze the loaf with beaten egg, then chill for 10 minutes. Bake for 30–40 minutes – do not open the oven door for at least the first 20 minutes of baking. Cool on a cake rack covered with a damp tea-towel – this gives a particularly nice shiny finish to the loaf.

Rye bread

275g dark rye flour
75g wholewheat flour
15g fresh yeast
1 tsp salt
250ml warm water

1 Put both types of flour in a mixing bowl and make a well in the centre. Dissolve the yeast in some of the water, pour it into the well, sprinkle with a little of the flour and allow to sponge. Mix the rest of the water with the salt, add to the mixture and work up to a dough. Form into a ball and leave to rise for about an hour, covered with a damp tea-towel. Knock down the dough, knead again

briefly and form into a round loaf. Sprinkle with flour and put on a baking sheet lined with non-stick baking paper. Allow to rise for about 20 minutes. Heat the oven to 220ºC/Gas 7 and put a roasting pan of water in the bottom of the oven.

2 Bake the loaf for about 50 minutes. Allow to cool on a cake rack.

The **extraction rate** of different flours varies considerably. Whole-wheat flour has the highest extraction rate. For this the whole grain is ground with the fibrous skin (bran). In Switzerland a light brown flour known as Ruchmehl is sold, which has an extraction rate of 82-85%. In Germany it is known as Type 1050.

Pear Bread from the Grisons

For 3 loaves

Filling:
400g dried pears, cut in small pieces
150g dried figs
125g sultanas
25g candied orange peel
125g walnuts
a pinch of cinnamon
25g candied lemon peel
125ml pear brandy
125ml rosewater

Brown bread dough:
15g yeast
150ml warm water
1 tsp salt
350g wholewheat flour

Yeast pastry:
1 tbsp salt
50g caster sugar
1 tsp malt
25g yeast
400ml milk
50g butter
650g plain white flour
1 egg yolk, to glaze

1 A day before you bake the bread, mix together the ingredients for the filling and chill for at least 15 hours.

2 For the brown bread dough, dissolve the yeast in the water. Mix the salt into the flour and add the dissolved yeast. Knead thoroughly until the dough is smooth and elastic, and no longer sticks to

Tips:
Fresh yeast works best at 22°C. All ingredients should be at room temperature.

Tip:
Do not slice the bread for at least 8 hours after baking.

Tip:
Pear bread keeps well.

190

your hands. Stir the filling ingredients into the dough and mix well. Cover the bowl with a damp teatowel and leave to rise in a warm place.

3 For the yeast pastry, dissolve the salt, sugar, malt and yeast in the milk in a large bowl. Mix in the flour and butter and knead it together to give a smooth pastry. Cut in 3 pieces and form each piece into a bolster about 16 cm long. Dust with flour and leave to rest wrapped in clingfilm for at least 1½ hours. Divide the filling into 3 parts and form them likewise into bolsters about 16cm long.

4 Roll out each piece of pastry to a rectangle about 20 x 40 cm. Brush the edges with water and place the bolster of dried fruit dough on top. Wrap the pastry around it, overlapping the edges slightly to seal. Put on a baking sheet lined with baking paper, seam sides underneath. Tuck the short ends under. Allow to rise for about 15 minutes. Heat the oven to 200ºC/Gas 6.

5 Glaze the pastry with egg yolk and prick all over with a fork. Bake for 45 minutes.

Rye Bread from Poschiavo

Malt or malt extract: a kind of sugar used by bakers as a dough improver. Available in all good bakeries. If necessary, can be replaced by brown sugar or honey, though the effect is less good.

For 2 loaves

600g rye flour, sifted
150g wholewheat flour
1 tbsp salt
25g yeast
½ litre lukewarm water

1 Put both sorts of flour in a large bowl. Mix in the salt. Make a well in the centre. Dissolve the yeast in the water and pour it into the well. Mix together and knead thoroughly to a firm, smooth dough. Cover with a damp cloth and leave to rise in a warm place for about an hour.

2 Cut the dough in half and shape into 2 round loaves. Make a hole in the middle with your finger, then draw out the dough to form a ring. Sprinkle with rye flour and put the loaves on a baking sheet lined with baking paper. Allow to rise for another 20 minutes.

3 Heat the oven to 230ºC/Gas 8. Slash the loaves in three places with a sharp knife and bake for 40–50 minutes.

Sherry Dressing

Tip: Sherry dressing can be made in large quantities and keeps well.

Makes about ¼ litre

3 tbsp sherry vinegar
3 tbsp stock
2½ tbsp Amontillado sherry
150ml sunflower oil
coarse salt, sugar, freshly ground pepper

1 Whisk together the vinegar, stock, sherry and oil until emulsified.

Herby Tomato Vinaigrette

Makes about 100ml

1 tbsp finely chopped stoned black olives
½ a tomato, peeled, halved, seeded and finely diced
½ a shallot, finely chopped
1 tbsp each red and yellow peppers, finely diced
3 sprigs parsley, chopped
a little fresh oregano, basil and marjoram, finely chopped
2 tbsp herb vinegar
4 tbsp safflower oil
salt and freshly ground pepper

1 Mix together all the ingredients and season to taste with salt and pepper.

Olive Oil Vinaigrette

Makes about 400ml

100ml raspberry vinegar
juice of ½ a lemon
a splash of Balsamic vinegar
300ml olive oil
salt and freshly ground pepper

1 Mix together all the ingredients until lightly emulsified.

Basic recipes

Light Veal Stock

Makes about ½ litre

200g veal bones, chopped small
700ml water
1 onion, peeled
1 leek, white part only
a piece of celeriac
a bouquet garni (bay leaf, cloves, crushed peppercorns, thyme)
salt

1 Blanch the bones, rinse under running water, drain and cool. Put them back in the pan with 700ml water, bring to a simmer, salt lightly and simmer for half an hour, skimming and degreasing regularly. Add the vegetables and bouquet garni and simmer for a further half hour. Strain carefully through muslin or a coffee filter paper.

Dark Veal (or Lamb) Stock

Makes about ½ litre

250g veal (or lamb) bones and trimmings
oil
50g assorted vegetables (onions, leeks, celeriac, carrots), finely diced
½ tbsp tomato purée
1 litre water
100ml white wine
a bouquet garni (bay leaf, marjoram, thyme, rosemary)
crushed peppercorns
salt

1 Fry the bones and trimmings gently in hot oil, add the vegetables and cook a little longer. Tip away any excess fat. Stir in the tomato purée and fry gently for a few minutes (be careful it does not burn, otherwise the sauce will be bitter). Splash in some of the water, each time allowing it to evaporate almost to a syrup. Repeat this process a couple of times. Moisten with wine, add the rest of the water, the bouquet garni and peppercorns and salt to taste. Bring to a boil and simmer for about an hour. Skim and degrease from time to time. Strain the sauce through muslin (or a coffee filter paper). Bring back to a boil and reduce to about half a litre. Taste for seasoning, adjusting if necessary.

Fish Stock

Makes about ¼ litre

200g fish trimmings (heads, bones etc.) from saltwater, white-fleshed fish
½ litre water
3 tbsp white wine
½ onion
a small piece celeriac, peeled
1 leek, white part only
3–4 tbsp mushroom trimmings
a bouquet garni (parsley stalks, bay leaf, some dill sprigs)
cloves, peppercorns
salt

1 Chop up the fish trimmings roughly and rinse them in cold water. Put them in a pan with the water, bring to a simmer and skim off any foam which rises. Add the wine, a little salt, the vegetables, bouquet garni and spices and simmer very gently for 30 minutes. Strain carefully through muslin or a coffee filter paper.

Pasta Dough (for Lasagne or Noodles)

Makes about 200g

150g strong white bread flour
1 egg + 2 yolks
1 tbsp oil
a pinch of salt

1 Sift the flour into a bowl. Add the remaining ingredients and work up to a smooth dough. Knead the dough thoroughly and let it rest for at least 1 hour before using.

Noodle Dough

Makes about 1kg

7 egg yolks
7 eggs
100ml oil
600g plain white flour
450g durum wheat flour

1 Beat together the egg yolks, eggs and oil. Mix in the flour and durum wheat flour and knead thoroughly. Form into a ball and chill. Any leftover bits of pasta can be frozen.

Tips: Noodle dough lends itself to many variations: for example, for rocket-flavoured noodles, cook some rocket leaves in a little stock, purée them and add 2 tbsp of the purée to the noodle dough.

Sweet Shortcrust Pastry with Egg White

For about 150g pastry

2 tbs brown sugar
1 egg white
75g plain white flour
50g butter

1 Mix together the sugar and egg white and leave to stand for 30 minutes. Rub the butter into the flour, add the egg white and sugar and work up to a dough. Chill for at least 1 hour.

Shortcrust Pastry

For about 750g pastry

500g plain white flour
2 level tsp salt
250g butter, cut in pieces
200ml water

1 Mix together thoroughly the flour, salt and butter until it resembles fine crumbs. Add the water and work up to a smooth dough. Chill for at least 1 hour.

Strudel Pastry

Makes about 250g

175g strong white bread flour
5 tbsp water
1 tbsp sunflower oil
1 tsp caster sugar
a pinch of salt

1 Sift the flour into a bowl, make a well in the centre. Add the water, oil, sugar and salt and gradually incorporate the flour from the sides. Mix to a firm dough, knead thoroughly till smooth and silky. Beat it several times on a floured table. Form into a ball and leave to rest at room temperature for 1 hour.

Rich Shortcrust Pastry with Egg White (for Pâtés)

Makes about 750g

400g plain white flour
1 level tsp salt
200g soft butter
125ml water
1 tbsp oil
1 egg white

1 Sift the flour with the salt onto a working surface and make a well in the centre. Add the butter in pieces. Mix together the water, oil and egg white and add them to the butter in the middle. Knead all the ingredients together to a smooth dough. Chill the dough for at least 12 hours before using.

Tip: Shortcrust pastry can be cut in portions and deep frozen, just like all pastries or pasta doughs.

Hollandaise Sauce

Makes about 100ml

100g butter
1 small shallot, chopped
8 peppercorns
a little vinegar
a little white wine
2 small egg yolks
juice of ¼ lemon
salt

1 Clarify the butter: heat it gently in a small pan until transparent, and the milky sediment sinks to the bottom. Keep the butter warm.
2 Boil the shallot and peppercorns with the vinegar and wine until reduced to about a third. Strain and put back in the pan. Add the egg yolks, and beat thoroughly with a wire whisk off the heat until the mixture begins to thicken. Gradually beat in the warm clarified butter, leaving behind the milky sediment. Season the sauce with lemon juice and salt.

Tip: Hollandaise sauce can be kept warm (not hot) until needed. If it gets too thick when you are adding the butter, whisk in a little cold water and continue beating.

Basic recipes

193

The Cook's private diary

CHAUREY
Maison fondée en 1840
EPERNAY

4.5. This one would be great
for the risotto with Sally + Chris

13.6. NEVER AGAIN!!!THAT'S IT! Amen!

14.9. In Sally's melon soup there was thyme, parsley, pepper and salt.

Recipe Index

SR 100

Facts & Figures

naturalgourmet on board

By the time this book is published, all Swissair flights originating in Zurich and Geneva will be serving naturalgourmet, from simple snacks to beer to complete menus. The market is not yet in a position to meet the high demand for organically-grown products. Thus at present, products are being purchased from organic sources and integrated production operations both in Switzerland and abroad:

33% organic products
57% products from integrated production
10% from conventional farming
(Status: October 1998)

Gate Gourmet in Zurich and Geneva, the catering operations of SAirRelations, supply Swissair with the naturalgourmet line. They have been certified for the processing of organic products by FIBL (Research Institute for Organic Farming) since the beginning and undergo regular inspections. The Gate Gourmet operations abroad are also inspected by independent, officially recognised authorities.

Addresses of Organic Farming Organisations

International Federation

IFOAM International Federation of Organic
Agriculture Movements, c/o Ökozentrum Imsbach
D-66636 Tholey-Theley
Tel. +49 6853 30 110, Fax +49 6853 30 110

Argentina

ARGENCERT
Bernardo de Irigoyen 760-10° B,
RA-1072 Buenos Aires
Tel. +54 1 334 2943, Fax +54 1 331 7185

Austria

Ernte für das Leben
Europaplatz 4, A-4020 Linz
Tel. +43 732 654 884, Fax +43 732 654 884 40

Belgium

Ecocert-Belgium
Ave. de L'Escrime, 85 Schermlaan,
B-1150 Brussels
Tel. +32 10 814 494, Fax +32 10 814 250

Canada

OCIA Saskatchewan Chapter I
Box 83 Socoro, CDN-Carlyle, SK S0G 0R0
Tel. & Fax +1 306 453 2884

France

Ecocert
Boîte postale 47, F-32600 L'Isle Jourdain
Tel. +33 5 6207 34 24, Fax +33 5 6207 11 67

Germany

Bioland-Verband für
Organisch-Biologischen Landbau
Postfach 349, D-73003 Göppingen
Tel. +49 7161 910 120, Fax +49 7161 910 127

Great Britain

Soil Association
86 Colston Street, GB-Bristol BS1 5BB
Tel. +44 117 929 0661, Fax +44 117 925 2504

Italy

AIAB Associazione Italiana per l'Agricultura
Biologica
Via Ponte Muratori 6, I-41058 Vignola (MO)
Tel. +39 59 763 774, Fax +39 59 764 287

Netherlands

SKAL
P.O. Box 384, NL-8000 AJ Zwolle
Tel. +31 38 422 6866, Fax +31 38 421 3063

Spain

CAE Comité d'Agricultura Ecologica Valenciana
Ing. Joachin Benlloch, 2-13° A, E-46006 Valencia
Tel. +34 6 373 7554, Fax +34 6 373 0631

Sweden

KRAV-Ekologish Kontrollföreningen för Ekologisk, Odling
Box 1940, S-75149 Uppsala
Tel. +46 18 100 290, Fax +46 18 100 366

Switzerland

Bio Suisse
Missionsstrasse 60, CH-4055 Basel
Tel. +41 61 385 9610, Fax +41 61 385 9611

U.S.A.

OCIA International
Organic Crop Improvement Association International
1001 Y Street, Suite B,
USA-Lincoln NE 68508-1172
Tel. +1 402 477 2323, Fax +1 402 477 4325

A selection of Swiss naturalgourmet producers

Bakery goods Hiestand AG, 8952 Schlieren;
Bertschi Bäckerei, Marktgasse 7/9, 8001 Zurich
Beer Brauerei Karl Locher AG, 9050 Appenzell
Eggs Lüchinger Schmid AG, 8302 Kloten
Meat and sausage Metzgerei Angst AG,
Herdernstrasse 61, 8040 Zurich; Metzgerei Ernst
Stettler, 4900 Langenthal; Traitafina AG,
5600 Lenzburg
Fruits and vegetables Tenti AG, Werkstrasse 16,
8400 Winterthur; Gastro-Star AG, 8108 Dällikon
Cheese Baer Interfromage, 6403 Küssnacht am Rigi;
Chäs Vreneli, Münsterhof, 8001 Zurich;
Emmi Käse AG, Habsburgerstrasse 12, 6002 Lucerne
Coffee Blaser Café, Guetstrasse 4, 3001 Berne
Various foodstuffs Biofarm-Genossenschaft,
4936 Kleindietwil
Jams Hero Schweiz AG, 5600 Lenzburg
Milk products Molkerei Forster, 9100 Herisau
Juices Biotta AG, 8274 Tägerwilen; Pomdor AG,
6210 Sursee
Chocolate Confiserie Sprüngli AG, 8953 Dietikon
Pasta Pasta Simone, 6572 Quartino
Terrines, ravioli and patés Rieder/Le Patron,
4461 Boeckten

Addresses of the recipe authors

Roland Jöhri

Jöhri's "Talvo", CH-7512 St. Moritz-Champfèr
Tel. +41 81 833 44 55, Fax +41 81 833 05 69

Anton Mosimann

"Mosimann's" London, 11B West Halkin Street,
Belgrave Square
GB-London SW 1X 8JL
Tel. +44 171 235 78 45, Fax +44 171 235 78 47

Wolfgang Kuchler

"Taverne zum Schäfli", CH-8556 Wigoltingen
Tel. +41 52 763 11 72, Fax +41 52 763 37 81

Peter Roth

"Kronenhalle Bar", Rämistrasse 4,
CH-8001 Zurich
Tel. +41 1 251 15 97 Bar,
+41 1 251 66 69 Restaurant

Rolf von Siebenthal

Gate Gourmet Zurich Ltd.,
CH-8058 Zurich-Airport
Tel. +41 1 812 61 10, Fax +41 1 812 91 92

Le Montreux Palace

Hotel Le Montreux Palace, Grand Rue 100,
CH-1820 Montreux
Tel. +41 21 962 12 12, Fax +41 21 962 17 17

Sprüngli

Confiserie Sprüngli, Paradeplatz,
CH-8022 Zurich
Tel. +41 1 221 17 22, Fax +41 1 211 34 35